HOUSEPLANTS FOR BEGINNERS

HOUSEPLANTS
FOR BEGINNERS

A Practical Guide to Choosing, Growing, and Helping Your Plants Thrive

Rebecca De La Paz

ROCKRIDGE
PRESS

Interior and Cover Designer: Scott Petrower
Art Producer: Sue Bischofberger
Editor: Emily Angell and Eun H. Jeong
Production Manager: Holly Haydash
Production Editor: Melissa Edeburn

Photography used under license from iStockphoto.com, cover and pp. ii, vi–vii, 2–3, 29, 31, 34–35, 42 (middle), 43 (bottom), 45, 46–47, 60, 65, 82, 88, 90, 92, 102, 104, 110, 114, 117, 119, 133, 137, 148, 154, 160, 171, 174–177, 179, 180, and 184; images used under license from shutterstock.com, pp. 8–9, 11, 18–19, 21, 27, 33, 37–41, 42 (top and bottom), 43 (top), 44, 56, 58, 59, 62–64, 66–81, 83, 86, 87, 89, 91, 93, 95–99, 101, 103, 105, 107–109, 111–113, 115, 116, 118, 120, 121, 123–132, 134–136, 138, 140, 145–147, 149–153, 155, 156, 158, 159, 161–166, 168–170, 172, 173, 178, 182, and 183; © Scenics & Science/Alamy Stock Photo, p. 61; © Gina Kelly/Alamy Stock Photo, p. 84; © Anna Yu/Alamy Stock Photo, p. 85; © blickwinkel/Alamy Stock Photo, pp. 94 and 181; © Lea Hughes/Alamy Stock Photo, p. 100; © Dorling Kindersley ltd/Alamy Stock Photo, pp. 106, 122, and 139; © Firdausiah Mamat/Getty Images, p. 141; © Organica/Alamy Stock Photo, p. 142; © Universal Images Group North America LLC/DeAgostini/Alamy Stock Photo, p. 143; © imagenavi/Getty Images, p. 144; © Florapix/Alamy Stock Photo, p. 157; © cbs/Alamy Stock Photo, p. 167; Leaf pattern © StatementGoods/DesignCuts.

ISBN: Print 978-1-64739-850-7 | eBook 978-1-64739-851-4
Ro

To the green thumbs who raised me,
shaped me, and encouraged me.

CONTENTS

INTRODUCTION

Welcome to the wonderful world of houseplants! The act of bringing home a plant is one of life's simplest pleasures, a treasure that never stops sparkling. Nature, especially in the outdoors, is an integral part of the human experience. But as we move into cities and get locked into a routine of walking from building to building, we fail to remember our need for nature. We forget what soft grass under our heads as we lie on a hillside feels like and how sweet breathing deeply among the trees can be. This disconnection from nature is a disconnection from who we really are and the life we were meant to experience. So how do we fix this problem? How can we remind ourselves of the importance of our nature connection and allow joy and healing?

Houseplants.

Typically prized more for their foliage than for their flowers, houseplants are any plants grown indoors. They are commonly "understory" plants—plants that grow along the bottom of the rainforest or forest floor. These plants can creep across the ground, grow up, or grow in trees. Because they don't require full sun, they are well suited for our homes.

My family members have always had houseplants. As a young adult, I wondered when I would receive my "special plant powers"—the green thumb that everyone else in my family seemed to possess naturally. Why wasn't I able to keep plants alive? Eventually I learned that a green thumb isn't an innate trait—it's the product of patience, time, and research.

Caring for houseplants has made me a forever learner. I have felt challenged to think differently and more deeply about something beyond my own life and circumstances. After taking the time to learn from and listen to my plants, I find that brown leaves appear less and less often.

This book is for the aspiring and curious indoor gardener. It presents all the information you need to succeed with houseplants. It will encourage you to *listen* to your plants, to *observe* them, and ultimately to *love* them. Part 1 will teach you how to shop for and pot plants as well as to choose the best place in your home for them. It covers strategies for a variety of challenges, including pests and diseases. Part 2 presents profiles of 120 houseplants grouped by level of maintenance, so you can familiarize yourself with plant needs and make the best plant choices for your lifestyle.

Now you know what took me years to learn: A green thumb is something to be cultivated, nurtured, and exercised. With this book you'll be able to enjoy the simple treasure that is houseplants.

PART ONE

HOUSEPLANTS 101

Caring for houseplants will open a world of new learning opportunities and add joy to your life. Let's learn about the history of houseplants and their benefits to humans as well as how to choose and pot plants, find the perfect perch for them in your home, and tackle a variety of challenges, including pests and diseases.

Chapter 1

THE BENEFITS OF HOUSEPLANTS

As humans, we have a profound connection to nature. Yet we spend most of our time indoors, at our computers, away from the flora and fauna that soothe our souls and minds. Enter houseplants, an easy way to bring the nature we crave indoors. Plants help us in innumerable ways: They provide stress relief, a creative outlet, and a boost of motivation, among many other benefits. This book will help you tap into the deep healing that occurs when you tend to your houseplants.

A BRIEF HISTORY OF HOUSEPLANTS

Houseplants weren't always houseplants—at one time, they were just plants. In some parts of the world, our houseplants are still just plants! When humans got involved and started to learn more about their unique capability to live indoors, houseplants were born. Whether to remind people of the outside world full of nature or to seemingly purify the air, humans have put houseplants to work for centuries.

The concept of keeping plants indoors can be dated back to ancient China, Egypt, and Rome. In ancient China, people practiced *penjing*, the recreation of realistic miniature landscapes, which inspired the Japanese art of bonsai. Over time, keeping tropical houseplants indoors was popularized, particularly as more and more plants were brought to Europe from the Caribbean beginning in the late fifteenth century.

Over the years, the practice of having houseplants has waxed and waned with the whims of interior designers and hobbyists alike. Whether during the boom in the Victorian era, when the Parlor Palm was popular, or in the 1970s and '90s, when the Snake Plant and Orchid were all the rage, fads arise every so often that acknowledge the value of bringing life indoors. In the 2010s and beyond, we've seen a surge of houseplant collectors because of the rise of apartment dwelling, our ever-growing relationship with technology and human-made objects, and a general disconnection from nature—today, house-plants are a way to hold on to nature. Thanks to social media, today's hopeful plant parents can scroll through plant Instagram pages, learn from plant YouTubers, and read blog after blog about everything houseplant. Regardless of style trends, once houseplants capture your heart, you will have a hard time ever going back to a life without plants.

What about houseplants has people collecting plant after plant until they are heavily outnumbered? Houseplants make beautiful ornaments and con-versation starters in the home, they stretch our knowledge of nature and the life within it, and, indeed, they do provide wonderful benefits for health and wellness.

THE BENEFITS OF BRINGING NATURE INSIDE

Bringing nature inside elevates our lives; flora and fauna have a way of transporting us to other, more pleasant places and reminding us what a gift life truly is. Houseplants are a wonderful way to boost spirits and ultimately get us connected again with nature.

Overall Health

Have you ever returned from a day at the beach, a walk in the woods, or a run in the park and felt a sense of relaxation? Studies have shown that spending time in nature lowers blood pressure and stress levels, enhances the immune system, lowers anxiety, and improves our mood. The science is clear—nature is good for us. But as cities have gotten larger and more developed, natural spaces have gotten smaller and smaller. Many people live with a nature deficit, where they could go days, weeks, or even months without stepping on a patch of grass or touching a leaf. This deficit has a negative effect on the mindset. Conversely, introducing houseplants into our homes allows us to bring nature indoors, so we can still experience the mental and physical health benefits of nature.

Outside our homes, many cities are working to maintain a nature balance in communities by designating "green space" and "blue space" to ensure that individuals still have access to nature in the city. Another change is the growing popularity of nature schools, where most of the day's lessons are taught outdoors. Houseplants and a growing need to "escape the city" are fueling a new movement of people looking to reconnect with nature.

Stress Levels

A popular place for indoor plants is offices, whether your workplace or dentist's office. That you see plants in these locations is not a coincidence—these places are where people are likely to experience high levels of stress, and houseplants are excellent stress relievers.

Another popular way to relieve stress is to do simple, mindless, repeatable tasks. Some folks take to knitting, others to houseplants. Houseplants give you an opportunity to work with your hands on a small, manageable scale. The repetitive activity of washing and dusting the leaves of a Swiss Cheese Plant or untangling the roots of a Golden Pothos has a way of teleporting us to our own world, far from life's stressors and obligations.

Air Quality

An experiment performed by NASA in 1989 revealed that a plant placed in a small, airtight chamber removed 70 percent of the toxins. This finding has been stretched and pulled in many directions, and ultimately resulted in the myth that having houseplants will improve the air quality in your home. Chances are, having a few houseplants in your home is not going to change the air quality as much as in a small, airtight container.

What might actually help the *feel* of your home, however, is your plants' transpiring. **Transpiration** happens when plants absorb moisture from the soil and eventually release this moisture into the air from their leaves. When you have a large collection of plants in close proximity, the ambient humidity will naturally be higher because of this process. In some parts of the world, ambient humidity can be as low as 5 to 10 percent. Running an air conditioner or heater has a tendency to dry out the air even further. Plants performing their normal task of transpiration will naturally bring up the humidity around them, and therefore provide more humidity for you and your home, if your collection is large enough.

Creativity, Motivation, and Happiness

Picking up a new hobby like indoor gardening is sure to spark several other complementary creative hobbies. You could try macramé. With just a few quick and easy knots, you'll have your own unique plant hanger. You could take a few pottery classes at a local studio to make planters for your houseplants. You might want to make pinch pots at home with clay that cures in the oven. Thrifting for older items that wouldn't normally be used for plants, like old milk cans, teapots, or colanders, is a fun way to create something brand new.

Taking care of houseplants can also help you feel more motivated and happier. You know those days when starting the day seems difficult or impossible? You might find those days much rarer when you have plants. Instead, start your day in a beautiful way, walking around and touching the plants' leaves, checking to see how everything is growing and what's needed, and watering your cactus and balcony herb garden outside, all while enjoying a cup of coffee. Plants don't necessarily provide instant gratification, but with time and patience, the small things we do for our plants make a big impact later. Pruning old leaves, repotting into fresh soil, dusting leaves, propagating to make new plants, and rearranging our indoor jungles are among the many mindless, simple tasks we take on when we own houseplants. This daily practice can set us on a positive course for the day, providing motivation for the less-fun tasks that may await.

After inviting a few houseplants into your home, you might notice your mood is a bit brighter. Houseplants have a way of reminding us to slow down, breathe, and stretch our limbs. There is nothing like the joy of finding a new leaf after you've been watching your plant patiently for months. This sense of accomplishment can leave you floating for the rest of the day and even week as you watch the plant push the leaf farther and farther. This delicate new leaf is a beautiful example of your plant's resilience and a sweet reward for you and your hard work.

Learning to communicate with something that cannot verbally speak to you can come with a steep learning curve, but seeing the fruits of your labor—sometimes literally—will motivate you to continue. You will almost certainly find joy in seeing you are capable of keeping plants alive. You *don't* have a brown thumb like you always thought! The truth is, if you take the time to truly understand your plants' needs, you will find success.

CONCLUSION

Whether you live in a dense city, a growing suburb, or on a large plot of land, you can enjoy houseplants. Cultivating a connection with nature is integral to the human experience—we crave grass under our toes, trees above our heads, and foliage beneath our fingers. There's a reason for this craving. We breathe easier among the trees. We smile at the beauty of flowers. Plants are an excuse to slow down, a reason to breathe, and an opportunity to learn.

Many people avoid taking on houseplants because they feel they don't know enough to help them succeed. In your plant journey, I encourage you to look for challenges. Sit with your plants and learn about them. Learn *from* them. And be patient with yourself—a green thumb doesn't happen overnight. To help your plants thrive, you'll need to absorb new information and listen to the cues from your plants. A thriving indoor jungle doesn't just happen; the process is methodical, requiring you to think deeply and strategically. In this place, you will find the most success with houseplants.

Starting an indoor jungle will revolutionize your life. Doing so will push you to think differently and live more intentionally. From their inception, houseplants were brought indoors to remind us of the outdoors and the healing properties of nature that we can't live without. You might find that your need for houseplants drives you to the garden center every weekend, where you walk around greenhouses and dream up all the possibilities. Not all houseplants are created equally; each plant will present you with unique challenges and quirks. Take the time to learn about them and you will find great success and happiness.

Chapter 2

CHOOSING AND BUYING YOUR HOUSEPLANT

One of the most inspiring parts about having a houseplant collection is visiting nurseries and greenhouses where they grow so beautifully. Upon opening the greenhouse doors, you are met with a sea of green leaves and warm air. You might find it difficult to keep yourself from touching every leaf, smelling every flower, and peering into every corner. Time spent in a greenhouse seems to never get old, no matter how many times you visit. In the winter, the greenhouse becomes an escape, a place to shed extra layers and drink in the sunlight and humidity, just like the plants. In the summer, these spaces burst with colors and textures to explore.

Whereas all plants are beautiful, some are better suited for certain environments. Understanding these factors will help you make better decisions for long-term success.

DON'T BE INTIMIDATED

Opening a greenhouse door and emerging into a potted jungle can be overwhelming. Seeing plants of so many different colors, shapes, and sizes can be a shock to the senses. Enjoy this moment and soak in everything you see, one plant at a time. Interact with plants that catch your eye; ask yourself why any particular one speaks to you. Touch their leaves, smell their flowers, pick up the plants and examine them. Choosing the perfect plant for your home shouldn't be a quick process, and requires intentionality to make sure all parties will be satisfied. The care labels might seem intimidating—*bright indirect light?* What do these instructions even mean? When you find yourself intimidated or overwhelmed, stop, take a deep breath, and simply enjoy being in this space. You start, of course, as a beginner, and all of this information will seem new, but before long you'll be strolling into a garden center knowing exactly what you can care for.

EVERY PLANT PARENT STARTS SOMEWHERE

You will be hard-pressed to find a plant person who hasn't killed a few plants in their lifetime—and that's a good thing to know. We're all learning, even sometimes the hard way. When you are out shopping for plants, you might find plants outside your skill level. You may be tempted to buy them because they are so beautiful, but chances are the situation won't end well for the plant. Start out with plants known for their hardiness to get practice. These first plants will teach you the lessons you need to become a better plant parent.

CONSIDER THESE FACTORS BEFORE YOU SHOP

Many people who fail at the beginning of their plant journey do not make intentional choices about the types of plants they can care for in their space. You may feel distracted and starstruck, but you'll want to think practically before you bring home any plant.

Where Will Your Plant Go?

Before you go plant shopping, look around your house and think about where you'd like to put a plant. Count how many open spaces you have. Some places to consider are on windowsills, on a coffee table in a bright room, on the bathroom counter, on your bedside table, hanging in a bright corner, or on a shelf in the kitchen. Many people like to integrate plants as a part of their decor. Generally, placing plants in high-visibility places is best so you don't forget about them.

Pinpoint the best spots in your home and take note of the conditions of that space, like what direction the windows face and the general humidity levels. Bring these notes with you to the garden center to compare to the care labels and talk with a nursery employee about what plants would do best in each spot.

HOW TO USE HANGING POTS FOR HOME DECOR

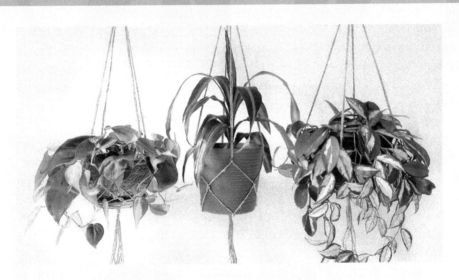

Making your own macramé hanger is simple, or you can purchase one from a local artist. Some plants that would do well in hanging baskets are Pothos (all), Heartleaf Philodendron, and Ivy. Smaller plants in pots 6 inches in diameter or smaller are better candidates for hanging baskets because they aren't as heavy. Likewise, hanging a plant in a ceramic pot will add extra weight, especially after a fresh watering. Instead, opt for a ceramic-looking plastic pot. If you are drilling into the ceiling to hang your plant, insert an anchor before you attach a C-hook, and grab a saucer so excess water doesn't drip on your floor.

What Kinds of Lighting Do You Get?

One of the most important factors in your home is lighting. With many plants, the direction that windows face is of the utmost importance. Take a look at your home and note what cardinal direction your windows face. Generally, south-facing windows will provide the strongest indoor light, west-facing windows bring hot afternoon light, east-facing windows provide cool morning light, and north-facing windows offer low ambient light throughout the day. Also take note of possible light obstructions like other buildings or trees. Certain plants will do better in certain windows depending on their light requirements and their proximity to the window. If you place a plant in direct sunlight, make sure to check for sunburn on the plant periodically (see page 51).

What's the General Temperature and Humidity?

Most houseplants, being from tropical and subtropical regions, don't tolerate low temperatures well. Typically, the lowest temperature they can comfortably handle is 55° Fahrenheit. If you keep a cool house or want to keep plants in a four-season sunroom, know that your houseplants could be negatively affected by low temperatures. Houseplants also don't take well to fluctuating temperatures and will drop leaves or stunt growth if constantly exposed to changing temperatures.

Depending on the types of plants you bring in, humidity is another important factor. Your home's natural ambient humidity will affect how well your plants grow, the type of growth they put out, and how often you see new leaves. For example, Hoya plants are okay living in a low-humidity environment, but you likely won't see tons of new growth. How quickly a plant can put out growth once they are placed in a humid environment is amazing.

Depending on where you live, you might already have suitable humidity for most plants. The weather app on your phone can tell you what the outside humidity levels are in your area, which is usually a good indication of your indoor humidity levels. Keep in mind that humidity in the home is almost always lower than outside, since air conditioners and heaters dry out the air. Another option is to purchase a hygrometer (a meter to measure humidity) to place in your plant spaces. Plants that need higher humidity are normally happy if the humidity is above 50 percent. Some examples of such humidity-loving plants are ferns, Anthurium plants, and any plant in the Marantaceae family. Boost humidity by keeping plants in a high-humidity room such as a bathroom with a window, purchasing a humidifier, placing plants close to one another for transpiration, or creating a humidity tray (see page 28).

What Size Plant Are You Looking For?

One of the best parts about plants is that they grow! The plant you see in the nursery could easily double or triple in size in the next year. Look at the growth habit of the plant when you are choosing plants to take home. Plants that grow upright will continue to get taller unless you cut them back. Trees, like the Fiddle-Leaf Fig, will grow bigger leaves and branch out in new directions. Larger plants oftentimes have a larger price tag than smaller plants. Purchasing just a few small plants to get started is totally fine, because in a few years, you will have nurtured them to double or triple their original size. If you opt for larger plants, you'll need more soil and larger pots.

The size of the plant also affects how often you'll need to water. Larger plants in big pots with lots of soil usually take longer to dry out. Smaller plants in small pots will often dry out quicker and may need more attention. This practice does vary and is also affected by how much light your plant gets, but, typically, the size of the plant does affect how often to water.

How Much Care Can You Give Your Plant? Be Honest.

The act of bringing home a houseplant is exciting; in fact, in their excitement, many people forget about the part where they have to keep the plant alive with regular care! You'll want to consider your personal schedule and the amount of time you are able to dedicate to your plants. If your schedule is busy, you probably won't fare well with houseplants that require more attention and frequent watering. Low-maintenance plants like Dracaena and Pothos will be your friend. If you have a more open schedule and the time to tend to your plants, your options are endless. Time is also a consideration when you think about how many plants you want. Buying more and more plants can be so easy, you may forget how much care each plant will need. As you progress in your plant hobby, you'll get into a groove of knowing how much time you have to spend on them.

What's Your Budget?

Houseplants are not typically expensive, but some have a higher price tag due to their inaccessibility and prestige among collectors. Start with simple plants with simple prices. Consider these your practice plants, and work your way up, if that feels right for you. Try not to get caught up in chasing after the "it" plant or the most "rare" plant, especially at first; these sorts of chases can quickly shift your mind away from the plants and how they make you feel, and make you focus more on the acquisition.

Having toxic plants around pets is possible because most pets don't really care about plants; however, if your pet has a history of eating plants, be sure to know the plant's toxicity level before buying it. When ingested, some plants can cause a strong reaction in the pet's gastro-intestinal tract all the way from mouth to stomach. Although cats seem to take more of an interest in chewing on houseplants, all pet owners should be aware of the toxicity level of their plants and protect their pets from toxic plants (see page 44). Even if a plant is labeled nontoxic, your pet could still experience problems from ingesting it; these problems just won't be serious or life-threatening. Following is a table of common toxic (not pet friendly) and nontoxic (pet friendly) houseplants. For more information on which plants are toxic and nontoxic to pets, visit the ASPCA website.

TOXIC AND NONTOXIC HOUSEPLANTS

10 TOXIC PLANTS	10 NONTOXIC PLANTS
Dumb Cane	Boston Fern
Fiddle-Leaf Fig	Chinese Money Plant
Hoya Hindu Rope	Heart Leaf Fern
Peace Lily	Moth Orchid
Philodendron (all)	Nerve Plant
Satin Pothos	Peperomia (all)
Snake Plant	Polka-Dot Plant
Swiss Cheese Plant	Red Prayer Plant
Syngonium Arrowhead Vine	Spider Plant
Umbrella Plant	Stromanthe Triostar

CHOOSING THE RIGHT PLANT FOR YOUR LIFESTYLE

If you have a busy lifestyle, you likely won't have time to keep up with watering every few days and should opt for more drought-tolerant plants. If you are more of a hands-on plant parent, you might benefit from taking on a plant that would enjoy the attention. By choosing plants that fit well into your lifestyle, you increase your chances of achieving long-term success with them.

Plant Shopping Cheat Sheet

The following table lists a few popular plants that require low-, medium-, or high-level care and attention.

LOW MAINTENANCE	MEDIUM MAINTENANCE	HIGH MAINTENANCE
Golden Pothos	Fiddle-Leaf Fig	Calathea Network
Snake Plant	Hoya Hindu Rope	Maidenhair Fern
ZZ	Watermelon Peperomia	Velvet Cardboard Anthurium

ASK FOR HELP!

One of the best ways to find information is through social media. Join in on hashtags or groups on social media platforms or watch videos from plant-centered YouTube channels. Local nursery employees are also a good source of information about plants specific to your region and their care. They can also provide tips and tricks catered to your home environment.

All that said, no plant advice can be taken as gospel. Every environment is different, with unique factors. The same plant living in neighboring homes can still act differently because no two conditions are identical. Instead, take the advice and adapt what you learn to work for your environment with your specific plant. Watch for the plant's cues when figuring out what to do to make the plant as happy as possible.

WHAT TO LOOK FOR

At nurseries, you'll often see multiple pots of one kind of plant. Which one should you choose? Your decision-making process should be informed by the following factors that consider the health of the plant.

Healthy Leaves

The leaves are often the first place the plant will communicate something is wrong. Some common leaf problems are brown tips, brown spots, yellowing, or curling. All these factors indicate the plant is responding to an unfavorable condition. None of these issues are severe, and you might also encounter them yourself at home. Nevertheless, try to find a plant with the fullest, healthiest leaves free of blemishes.

The leaves and stems can tell you a lot about how much attention a plant will need. Thicker, more succulent leaves with thicker stems indicate the plant is more drought tolerant. The plant holds water in these places, so no need to water as often. Thin leaves (think paper) with skinny stems will need to be watered more often because their leaves cannot hold as much water.

Full Shape

Is the plant leggy and stringy or full and round? Some plants grow long and stringy branches as a result of low light, or when searching for something to climb onto. Try to find plants that are full in their pots. Depending on growth habit, this fullness will fluctuate from plant to plant.

Strong Stem

For trees and other upright-growing houseplants, check that the main stem is sturdy. Has the nursery braced the stem with a pole? Is the plant hanging over and bending? A strong stem is a great indication of a healthy plant that will be able to support new growth.

New Growth

Greenhouses provide a plant's most ideal indoor conditions. If you don't see new growth coming in in the greenhouse, especially during the growing season, something else might be going wrong. New growth won't always be freshly popping out, but check the newest leaves to see how new they are. New leaves are typically a lighter green color than the rest of the plant, generally smaller, and much softer. The oldest leaves are darker and very sturdy.

Pest-Free

Pests often find their way into our homes aboard a new plant. To check for pests, look closely at the undersides of the leaves along the veins or at the petiole where the leaf meets the stem. Hold the plant up to direct light to check for any fine webbing or white or red spots in these places. Performing this check doesn't guarantee bringing home a pest-free plant, though, because certain pests could still be in the larval stage. In general, you'll want to isolate new plants for a few weeks (away from other plants) when you first bring them home in case there were any additional travelers.

ASK YOURSELF WHETHER YOU LOVE THE PLANT

Just like with anything else you buy, you'll want to ask yourself, "Do I really love this plant?" If you are hesitant or just buying that plant because you want to buy a plant, chances are you will wind up regretting your purchase. The excitement of new plants does wear off once you find a pest, leaves drop, or a brown spot develops. If the plant is what you really love, you'll be more willing to make changes to figure out what's gone wrong. If you don't like the plant anymore, chances are you'll let it slowly die. To avoid wasting your time and money, spend an extra moment before you purchase a plant to decide if you really need and like it.

CONCLUSION

Greenhouses are sometimes the closest we'll get to being in a tropical place. As you discover the joy, you might find yourself running to the local greenhouse on your lunch break just to breathe in the warm, moist air and take in all of the plants. These spaces can be a place of refuge, renewal, and excitement. In the midst of all the excitement, we still want to make sound decisions. Some plants are wonderful to visit at the nursery, but difficult to take care of when you bring them home. As you grow in your plant journey and collection, you'll begin to create a mental list of plants great for visiting, but not great for taking. My hope is that whether or not you bring something home, each time you visit a greenhouse you feel a sense of awe for the life held within.

Chapter 3

BRINGING YOUR NEW HOUSEPLANT HOME

The possibilities of a new plant are endless, and you're just getting started! Finding the perfect pot and learning how to help your plant thrive long term are important first steps of plant parenthood.

CHOOSING THE RIGHT POT

Now that you have brought home your new houseplant, it is time to find it the best pot to grow in. Choosing a pot for your plant is similar to picking out a home for yourself. The container should be the correct size, made from the right materials, and have room to grow. The best way to set your plant up for success is to provide the best home possible.

When selecting a pot, you'll need one that's the right size. Big plants don't always need big containers; rather, pot fit should be based on the size of the roots, not the amount or size of leaves. For a right-size pot, pull the plant from the nursery container to see the root development. A lot of roots wrapping around the soil ball is an indication the root system is highly developed and the plant needs a pot no more than 2 inches larger than the nursery one. If the root system is not developed and you see more soil than roots, choose a pot of the same size as the nursery container, or possibly 2 inches smaller.

Different Types of Pots: Plastic vs. Ceramic vs. Terra-Cotta

No one material is superior to another; rather, they each serve a different function with different capabilities. The most common pot material is plastic, which is what you'll see at most nurseries. These pots have many drainage holes at the bottom, are soft enough to bend for easy repotting, and are the lightest of all pot options, making them perfect for hanging planters. For long-term potting, choose sturdier plastic.

Next is terra-cotta, which means "baked earth" in Italian. Terra-cotta pots are often left unglazed, giving them porous, moisture-wicking capabilities. Best identified by their orange hue, terra-cotta pots are affordable and wonderful for heavy-handed waterers, because the porous clay allows for excess water to be absorbed and drained. Plants that enjoy drying out between waterings are excellent matches for terra-cotta pots.

Ceramic pots come in many colors, shapes, sizes, and designs, ideal for style-minded indoor gardeners. They hold moisture similarly to a plastic pot and are great for plants that like to stay moist for longer.

The Importance of Drainage

Often overlooked, but extremely important, is the drainage hole. The drainage hole allows excess water and minerals to be flushed out every time you water. If your pot doesn't have a drainage hole, use it as a cover—just place a plastic pot with drainage inside the pot and remove the plastic one for watering. Make sure all the water has emptied out before you put the plastic pot back in the cover pot. Drilling your own drainage hole is another option (see page 23).

To keep furniture and surfaces protected, buy a matching saucer to catch excess water, or use an old plate.

WHEN AND HOW TO REPOT

When plants have outgrown their pots, they'll need to be repotted, typically every one to two years. Signs that a plant needs a new pot include:

- Stunted new growth
- Roots poking out the top or bottom of the pot
- Soil drying out more quickly than usual
- Yellowing leaves

These signs may indicate the plant is root-bound, meaning there are more roots in the pot than soil. Consequently, the plant isn't receiving proper nutrients and moisture retention to continue growing well.

Another time you would repot a plant is fresh from the nursery, when potting into a new, permanent home. Here's how:

1. To remove a plant from a plastic pot, turn the plant on the side and squeeze the pot. Gently grab the base of the plant and pull as you squeeze. If you're repotting from a ceramic or terra-cotta pot, lay the plant on the side and gently tap the pot onto the surface to loosen the soil. Soak terra-cotta pots in water for a few minutes to help loosen the roots from the clay. With a combination of tapping, gentle pulling, and pushing up from the drainage hole, the plant should slide out. Do this work outside or inside on a repotting tarp, newspaper, or towel.

2. Next, loosen the **root ball** with your fingers to allow the plant to acclimate. Don't be afraid to get your hands dirty–the looser you can get the root ball, the better. Take this time to remove any yellowing, dead, or decaying leaves from the plant for a fresh start.

3. Fill in the bottom of your new pot with potting mixture. Add a piece of broken terra-cotta pot, netting, or window screen to prevent soil from falling out of the drainage hole. Only fill the bottom one-third with soil, or you'll run the risk of the plant retaining too much moisture and developing root rot.

4. Place your plant in the center of the pot and backfill soil in the remaining space. Leave about half an inch at the top of the pot so the soil won't overflow when you water the plant.

5. Gently press down on the soil to remove any large air bubbles. Another way to help the soil settle is by gently tapping the pot on the work surface. Give your plant a drink of water and place it in the perfect spot!

Decorative pots can enhance the aesthetics of your home, bringing in pops of color. Many decorative pots don't start out as great homes for our plants, but you can easily amend a pot to the plant's liking. For starters, not all decorative pots have drainage holes. To create one, make an "X" on the bottom of your pot with masking tape and carefully drill a hole in the center with a diamond-tip drill bit. Alternatively, use the decorative pot as a cover. Simply place an already-potted plant into the decorative one and remove the inner pot whenever you need to water.

DIFFERENT TYPES OF POTTING MIXES FOR DIFFERENT TYPES OF PLANTS

The type of soil you choose for your plant depends mostly on how much moisture retention the plant needs. Every houseplant needs a well-draining soil mixture so the water will drain through the pot quickly without pooling or settling at the top of the soil. The best soil match for your plant will help ensure you grow a healthy plant from roots to leaf tips.

Choose Your Soil Wisely

Before you bring a plant home, find out the plant's moisture retention needs and choose a soil accordingly. Some plants, like Calathea or ferns, like their soil to stay moist longer and tend not to do well when their soil dries out too quickly. A soil mixture for ferns should be entirely different than one for cacti, which can't live under extended moist conditions.

Soil is made up of a mixture of compost, or decomposed organic matter, and additives such as pumice, perlite, orchid bark, vermiculite, coco chips, and coco peat (an eco-alternative to peat moss).

Buying a Ready-Made Soil Mix

At the garden center, you'll find a wide variety of ready-made potting mixes. When choosing a soil mixture for your houseplants, look for one formulated for the types of plants you are potting. You wouldn't use a garden mix alone on houseplants because they are typically too heavy in peat moss, which is also bad for the environment—coco peat is a better alternative. Tropical houseplant mixes usually include root-aerating additives such as perlite, pumice, bark, or coco chips, which help the soil dry out faster or drain quicker.

Creating Your Own Custom Soil Mix

Creating your own custom soil mix isn't difficult and offers more control over how well your soil drains and retains moisture. Let's review some types of soil additives and their features.

SOIL ADDITIVES		
ADDITIVE	MATERIAL	PROS/CONS
Coco chips	Larger chunks of coconut husks	Great for adding chunkiness, drainage, and moisture retention; takes many years to break down.
Coco peat	A recycled by-product of coconut	Eco-friendly alternative to peat moss; helps soil retain moisture.
Orchid bark	Typically fir bark	Provides aeration for roots and ideal for **epiphytes**; great for a chunky texture; depending on the size of the chips, orchid bark can break down in the soil.
Perlite	Lightweight volcanic glass	Similar to polystyrene, perlite sometimes floats to the top of the soil. Can also be used for propagation.
Pumice	Porous volcanic glass	Highly porous, pumice is great for holding water and air and achieving a "chunky" texture.
Vermiculite	A heat-expanded silica material	Excellent for moisture retention, vermiculite is useful for propagating and seed starting.

Because many plants have similar soil needs, create a basic mix that will work for the majority of your plants, then adjust, if needed, on a plant-by-plant basis. Use a general potting soil or compost and additives of your choosing. Mix in a bowl or container and examine. Can you clearly see your additive in the mixture? If not, try adding a handful more. Test how well your soil drains by scooping some into a pot and watering at the sink. If the water pools at the top, add more additive. Be creative and try using more than one additive. Many serve similar purposes, but others help in unique ways. You'll find which additives work best with your plants.

THE IMPORTANCE OF FERTILIZING YOUR PLANT

Fertilizer works similarly for plants as vitamins do for humans. Plants use the nutrients in the soil; therefore, soil loses nutrients over time. Fertilizing replaces those nutrients. If you avoid fertilizing, eventually your plants will only produce new growth once in a while, or not at all. Fertilization gives your plant an extra boost to continue putting out beautiful new growth that is bigger every time. If your plant is freshly repotted, you won't need to fertilize right away.

Common Plant Fertilizers

Fertilizers include liquid, powder, granules, and organic or synthetic varieties. They are made of a ratio of nitrogen, phosphorus, and potassium called the NPK ratio, shown in three numbers with dashes in between. For example, a 10-10-10 fertilizer contains 10 percent nitrogen, 10 percent phosphorus, and 10 percent potassium. These are the key ingredients in fertilizers, though other ingredients may also be present.

Organic Fertilizer

Organic fertilizer comprises organic and natural material from plants or animals, such as compost, seaweed, animal manure, fish emulsion, and more. It's ideal because slow-releasing, organic fertilizer, as the term suggests, brings more organic material into the soil. Though not as fast-acting as synthetic, organic fertilizer improves long-term soil health. On the downside, organic materials do not always have a pleasant smell.

Synthetic Fertilizer

Synthetic fertilizers are made up of synthetically produced nitrogen, phosphorus, and potassium. They contain close to the perfect ratio for your houseplants and are often affordable. Synthetic fertilizer works faster than organic types and comes in liquid and granule forms. Granules are a slow-release method that allows a little bit of fertilizer into the soil with each watering.

HOUSEHOLD SCRAPS FOR PLANTS

Compost is the organic matter in your soil that helps your plant receive nutrients. Create your own compost at home by using kitchen and household scraps that will turn into a great organic fertilizer for your plants. Once the compost is fully decomposed, sprinkle it on top of your soil; then water to feed the plant. Composting is also a great way to reduce or use waste.

The three components of composting are browns—leaves, sticks, and grass clippings; greens—fruit and vegetable scraps, eggshells, and coffee grounds; and water. Avoid composting items like meat scraps, dairy products, and pet waste. To start a compost bin indoors:

1. Purchase or make a small compost bin with holes to help the compost breathe, because air is an important part of proper decomposition.

2. Add a charcoal filter to help prevent odors and flies.

3. Alternate greens and browns layer by layer in your compost pile.

4. Moisten dry materials as you add them. If you don't want to use the compost yourself, plenty of places, like community gardens, will take your compost for others to use.

5. The amount of time compost takes to start breaking down into soil—from as little as 3 to 4 weeks to as much as a few years—depends on the size and contents of the pile. The compost is ready when you see more soil than rotting vegetables.

PROPAGATING PLANTS: SIMPLE STEPS TO GROW A NEW PLANT AND THE THREE BEST PLANTS TO USE

Propagating, or creating new plants from existing plant matter, is a wonderful way to make more plants for free. How you **propagate** a plant depends on the plant type; some plants propagate via stem cutting, others by leaf cutting, and most by cutting between stems and aerial roots. Most plants will propagate well in water, but experiment as well with rooting plants in moss, perlite, soil, or vermiculite, all readily available in garden centers. Research your specific plant to determine which method is most effective for growing new leaves.

Leaf cuttings: The most common plant that propagates from leaf cuttings is the Dracaena, commonly known as the Snake Plant. Cut the leaf into two- or three-inch segments and place in soil, water, vermiculite, or perlite. In a few weeks to a month, a small leaf spike should grow up through the surface. Keep the leaf cutting in this soil until the roots have filled the container, then repot.

Nodes or aerial roots: The most common plant that propagates by **node** or aerial (above the ground) root is Pothos. Simply cut between the aerial roots and place in moss or water. Eventually, you will see thick and fuzzy white roots.

Stem cuttings: The most common plant that propagates from stem cuttings is Peperomia; simply cut along the leaf stem and place in water. Soon the cutting will produce roots and eventually baby leaves. The mother leaf will die off after she is exhausted.

When and How to Fertilize

You'll only want to fertilize your plants during the growing season—typically, spring, summer, and fall. If you live in a warmer climate, your plants might grow throughout the winter season. As long as the plant is producing new growth, fertilize. Generally, you'll want to fertilize every 2 weeks to once a month, depending on your fertilizer. The instructions on the package will tell you how often to fertilize.

Fertilizers are uniquely formulated, so, again, read the package for directions. Liquid fertilizers need to be diluted in water, usually by the gallon; granule slow-release fertilizer is mixed into the potting soil or sprinkled on top; and organic fertilizers are sprinkled on top.

DECIDING WHERE TO PUT YOUR PLANT

Proper placement helps ensure that the plant grows the best it can. Some plants need greater light, more humidity, and/or warmer temperatures than others. Consider where these factors might be best before bringing a plant home.

Humidity

Tropical plants are accustomed to tropical environments, which includes a lot of humidity. Humidity above 40 percent is ideal. Most houseplants will thrive in high levels of humidity, so you don't really have to worry about the humidity being too high. Conversely, many plants will do poorly in low-humidity environments. Read up on the humidity requirements before you bring home any plant, because it can be tricky to raise the humidity in your home. Supplement with humidifiers, place humidity-loving plants in the bathroom or near the kitchen sink where humidity is higher, or create a humidity tray. Fill a deep plastic saucer or plate with pebbles and water. Set the plant atop the filled tray, making sure the water level doesn't reach the pot. The saucer or plate should be wider than the pot.

Another option is to purchase an inexpensive hygrometer to gauge the humidity levels in your home and help you decide where to put your plants.

Light

Your home can provide four types of light:

1. Ambient sun in a north-facing window

2. Cool, bright sun in an east-facing window

3. Warm, bright sun in a west-facing window

4. Hot, bright sun in a south-facing window

Before you place your plant in a window, read about its light requirements. Bringing a plant closer to the window will provide more intense and possibly direct light, while bringing it away from the window will provide softer, lower light. As long as there is decent light, most houseplants will be perfectly happy with the light achievable in the home, so there's no need to put them in direct sun outside—in fact, many houseplants wouldn't like direct sun outside.

Tender foliage will often develop brown or black spots due to sunburn. Remember that houseplants are typically understory plants in the jungle, so they aren't accustomed to full sun or even large amounts of sun inside.

The amount of light that a plant receives will also affect how quickly the soil is able to dry out. Plants that sit in a hot windowsill will dry out faster because they are using more water to stay hydrated. Additionally, the higher temperature causes the soil to dry out faster. Plants that sit in a darker corner of the house are using less resources and will naturally sit in moist soil longer.

Temperature

Typically, the lowest temperature that houseplants can stand is 55 degrees Fahrenheit. Be aware of the conditions of your plants, especially if they are sitting on drafty windowsills or on a covered patio. If you are experiencing temperatures lower than 55 degrees Fahrenheit, monitor these plants to ensure they don't suffer from cold damage.

WATERING

One of the biggest mistakes new plant parents make is watering their plants too often, not enough, or altogether incorrectly. By watering your plants the right way, you'll ensure their long life and your ultimate joy.

Look at your soil like a sponge. When you start to do dishes with a dry sponge, it takes a few moments for the sponge to be able to soak up the water. When some time has passed since the last watering, soil tends to get hard and won't absorb moisture immediately. You might notice that dry soil has pulled away from the edges of the pot. For the soil to be able to absorb moisture, you must completely saturate it. Deeply watering your plant ensures that every bit of soil is moist; therefore, all the roots will be able to absorb moisture.

There are several techniques for watering plants: watering from above, watering from below, and wick watering.

Bottom Watering

Some plants have tender foliage that prefers not to get wet, like African Violets. These types of plants can be bottom watered. Bottom watering is also a great way to water plants that have hardened soil. To bottom water, fill a container, sink, or tub with a few inches of water and place the potted plant inside. The water will eventually soak up into the soil. This process is helped by capillary action, which helps the roots absorb moisture and move it up to the stems and leaves. Leave your plant in the water until the topsoil is moist. Bottom-watered plants still must be watered from the top every 2 or 3 waterings to flush out built-up salts and minerals in the soil.

Top Watering

Watering from above requires you to add water to the top of the pot until it drains out the bottom. When the soil is hardened, the water may run off to the edges of the pot and straight out of the drainage hole. To help the soil soak up water quicker, loosen the topsoil or gently poke holes with chopsticks, a knitting needle, or your fingers.

Wick Watering

Wick watering involves wrapping a wick such as an old shoelace or cotton cord around the root ball of the plant and leaving a tail out of the drainage hole. The tail must be long enough to reach a cup of water so it can soak it up and deliver it to the plant. This technique also makes use of capillary action. Wick watering is great for low-maintenance watering, because this technique allows a more passive environment for you and your plant. Wick-watered plants should still be watered from the top occasionally to flush out salts and minerals.

How Much Water Is Too Much?

There is no such thing as giving your plant too much water at one time. As long as your soil is well draining, the water will continue to move through the drainage hole and will not negatively affect the plant or its roots. The concept of "too much water" comes from watering too *frequently*. Overwatering happens over time. When a plant's roots are constantly wet, they don't have the chance to breathe; this reason is why most plants like to dry out at least a little bit between waterings.

Signs of Overwatering and Underwatering

An overwatered plant is one that hasn't been allowed to dry out between waterings. This practice leads to root rot, a condition in which the roots turn mushy and dark brown to black. Most healthy roots are white. An overwatered plant will also yellow off its leaves. Moist soil, yellowing leaves, and a drooping plant, even a few days after watering, is a sign of overwatering and likely root rot (see page 43 for treatment). Avoid this deadly condition by letting your plant dry out between waterings, as well as providing the correct drainage in the soil.

An underwatered plant is a plant left without water for too long. Signs of underwatering, or a thirsty plant in general, are drooping leaves, uncharacteristically soft and bendy leaves, as well as yellowing leaves in more serious cases. Our plants are great communicators of their watering needs. When your plant begins to droop or you are able to bend a leaf you couldn't before, it's time for a deep watering.

GROOMING LEAVES

One of the most therapeutic parts of having plants is washing their leaves, and there's good reason for this ceremony. When plants get water on their leaves, it can leave behind white spots. They also will collect dust after a while. Excess dust prevents plants from photosynthesizing. A regular routine of washing your leaves can help, and doing so gets you in the habit of checking for pests. You can buy commercial leaf shines or make a DIY mixture with 1 part citrus juice and 1 part water. Using a microfiber cloth, gently wash each leaf with this mixture and see how much more beautiful they are after a quick clean and shine. Another option is to bring your plants into the shower and rinse them with water; just wash them off with your leaf-shining mixture afterward.

Removing old, ugly, or yellowing leaves can also help your plant put its energy into new leaves. However, old or yellowing leaves won't hurt the plant, so the choice is yours to keep or remove them.

PLANTING FROM A SEED

Starting plants from seed allows you to observe a plant growing through all its stages. Vegetables and flowers are the most common plants to grow from seed because their germination process is so fast. Purchasing seeds from a reputable seller allows you to grow houseplants from seed.

Step-by-Step Instructions for Seed Starting

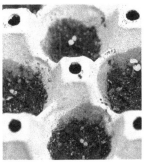

1. **Prepare your container.** One of the easiest containers in which to grow plants from seed is egg cartons; just punch small drainage holes in the bottom before planting the seeds.

2. **Buy the right soil.** Purchase soil specific to seed starting and pre-moisten before placing in the container.

3. **Plant your seeds.** For best results, plant a few seeds per cell. Some seeds might not come up at all, but if both seeds in the cell germinate, cut off one of them.

4. **Let there be light.** The most important part for seedling success is a lot of light. Place your seedlings in a bright windowsill (south-facing is great), or a few inches from a grow light.

5. **Water gently.** Mist the soil and allow to slightly dry out between waterings.

6. **Fertilize.** Seedling soil doesn't have many nutrients, so you'll need to fertilize the seedlings with a gentle organic fertilizer when you water.

7. **Repot and label.** After your seedlings have grown for at least 6 weeks, check to see if they're ready for repotting. You'll know when the roots have started to encapsulate the soil and wrap around themselves. Repot the seedlings into larger containers and label them so they don't get mixed up.

CONCLUSION

This chapter's lessons are some of the most important for houseplants. By implementing this knowledge, you are sure to have houseplant success. If you don't right away, don't give up! Learning to take care of houseplants is a long-term journey and takes trial and error. Succeeding with houseplants requires good observational skills. You might not immediately see the results you'd like, but with time, you will. Your plants will tell you when they are thirsty, when they need extra fertilizer, and whether they like their home. Keep developing that keen eye so you're able to recognize the signs. As a living being, your plant has a life, too, and won't always do what you want, and that's okay. One day soon, watering your plants, trimming them back, or repotting them will feel like second nature.

Chapter 4

PESTS, DISEASE, AND OTHER HOUSEPLANT CHALLENGES

Pests and disease are inevitable aspects of owning houseplants. Naturally, houseplants aren't as affected by pests as outside plants, but one of the most common ways pests enter our homes is through new plants. Houseplant disease can be confusing, but soon enough, you'll be a pro at knowing what to do.

PLANT SICKNESS

Houseplants have a few ways of telling us they have a disease or pest; a keen eye will help you spot something wrong. Once you have a plant for a while, you know how new growth should look when coming in and what color the leaves typically are, so you'll notice when something is "off." When you sense a problem, check the plant right away for a pest or disease. Pests can be covert and require you to look closely and know what you are looking for. The best place to start your search for pests is around new growth; pests enjoy congregating around new growth, and as a result, the growth can be misshapen. Pests also enjoy living along the petioles, where the leaf meets the stem, or along the veins of the leaves in the hard-to-reach grooves.

Most houseplant problems are treatable—many can be helped just by using household products like rubbing alcohol, hydrogen peroxide, dish soap, and water. For more serious infestations, seek out a chemical insecticide or fungicide, and for more natural methods, try out beneficial insects like ladybugs and green lacewings.

COMMON HOUSEPLANT PESTS

Finding pests on your houseplants is a normal experience all plant parents will go through, so you'll want the tools and knowledge to combat them. As soon as you discover a pest in your plant, move the plant away from all others. Pests can transfer to other plants, especially when their foliage is touching. For best success getting rid of a houseplant pest, you'll need to understand the lifecycle of the pest you are working with. Many pests lay hundreds of eggs *a day* so you must target the pest at all life stages. Treat your plants with your chosen method for 3 days straight, wait for 5 days, then treat for another 3 days. Eggs normally take around 5 days to hatch, so if there is a second wave of pests coming, you'll eliminate them with the second treatment. Let's take a look at some of the most common houseplant pests.

Aphids

Aphids are a soft-bodied insect that give birth to live insects. They do not typically fly but will do so if the population is overcrowded. They are most usually light green, pear-shaped, and visible to the naked eye, but can also be yellow, brown, red, or black. Aphids are a common pest for outdoor plants, but they can make their way indoors as well. Aphids congregate in large groups, making them very easy to see. By using their mouthparts, they suck the juices from the plant and leave behind a wilted, limp specimen.

Treatment: Aphids are easy to blast off your plant by spraying the stem and leaves with water from a hose outside. Turn the plant on the side when you spray to make sure the aphids don't land in the soil. For best results, follow by washing the plant with warm, soapy water along the stems and leaves. Ladybugs and ladybug larvae are excellent natural predators for aphids.

Fungus Gnats

Fungus gnats are small black flies that congregate in the soil. They are more annoying for you than they are harmful to your plants. They feed on the organic material in soil and can enter your home with contaminated soil. You'll see fungus gnats popping up in soil that has stayed too wet for too long. Female fungus gnats lay eggs in the top 2 inches of soil and multiply quickly.

Treatment: To remove fungus gnats effectively, target the larvae as well as the adults by using a mixture of 1 part hydrogen peroxide and 2 parts water to water the soil. Hydrogen peroxide has no negative effect on your soil or the plant and is effective in removing all living matter in the soil. This condition isn't always ideal, considering this mixture also kills microbes, but soil conditioners can get your soil back in shape.

To capture the adults, set up yellow sticky traps—small, yellow sticky papers that attach to garden stakes—in the soil of affected plants. These traps are sold at garden centers and online. Another option is making a mixture of apple cider vinegar, water, and dish soap and placing it near affected plants. Changes may take a few days to come, but soon you will find your sticky traps filled and fewer gnats flying around. As an alternative and a preventative measure, let at least the top 2 inches of your soil dry out for all plants; doing so will create a less-ideal environment for gnats to congregate and reproduce.

Mealybugs

Mealybugs are a white, soft-bodied insect, sometimes with long tails, that use their mouthparts to suck the juices from the plant. They are easily visible to the naked eye due to their white color and egg sacs that resemble cotton. Mealybugs can lay up to 600 eggs at a time, so they multiply quickly. They congregate in hard-to-reach crevices of houseplants and under the leaves along the veins. Mealybugs take a special interest in succulent-like plants that have plenty of juice for them to drink.

Treatment: Mealybugs are simple to remove by spraying with water or using a cotton swab covered in rubbing alcohol. These pests will die on impact. Once you've removed all visible mealybugs, spray the plant with insecticidal soap, neem oil (an organic pesticide), or an insecticide labeled as effective for mealybugs. Green lacewings are an effective insect to eradicate mealybugs.

Scale

Scale is a brown, armored pest that blends in with your plant and can easily go undetected. This pest congregates along the stems and veins of the plant and doesn't move once in adult form. Adult scale insects lay eggs that later hatch and are able to walk until they find their final spot.

Treatment: The only way to remove this armored pest is by physically scraping it off with a fingernail, cotton swab, or other object. Because of the pest's armor, a spraying product is ineffective. Once you have scraped off the scale and ensured these pests didn't fall into the soil, spray your plant with a mixture of water, dish soap, and rubbing alcohol. Make sure you're not inadvertently trying to peel off an aerial root or non-pest-related bump along the stem.

Spider Mites

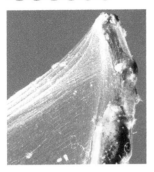

Spider mites are microscopic red or green mites (arachnids) that can lay up to 100 eggs at a time. Spider mite damage looks like yellow or brown dots all over the leaves, but you might notice their webs first. Spider mites create webs along the underside of the leaves, petioles, and even the front of the leaves. These spots are where they lay their eggs. You can see the webs by holding the plant up to light or misting the leaves. Though all plants are vulnerable to a spider mite infestation, they are commonly found on Alocasia and Syngonium plants.

Treatment: Start by spraying the leaves with water from a hose outside to remove adults and disrupt their webs. Next, make a mixture of 1 part rubbing alcohol, 1 squirt of dish soap, and 3 parts water, and wash or scrub the leaves. Wash carefully along the veins of the leaves and along the petioles. Another option is to mix in an organic or granule-based systemic insecticide, which will allow the plant to take up the insecticide and kill the pests when they feed on the plant. For serious infestations, use a chemical insecticide labeled as effective against spider mites. Green lacewings are beneficial insects for removing spider mites.

Thrips

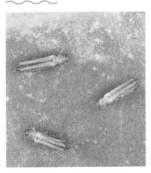

Thrips are long, soft-bodied insects barely visible to the human eye. Sometimes the only evidence of these pests are their droppings, which can look like wood shavings. Thrips produce eggs that hatch within a few days. At this point, they begin feeding on the plant, using their mouthparts to suck the juices from the plant and scrape the leaves. You might notice that your thrips-infested plant takes on a pale silvery-blue hue. Thrips are a tough pest to completely eradicate because they fly and spread quickly.

Treatment: Because thrips are aggressive and hard to contain, home remedies might not be as effective. However, spraying the plant with a mixture of 1 part rubbing alcohol, 2 parts water, and a few squirts of dish soap can help. Chemical insecticides, effective in removing thrips, are a great solution. Another just as effective option would be a systemic solution that you give to the plant when watering. Plants pull in these solutions, killing the pest when it punctures the plant. Thrip predators and minute pirate bugs are beneficial insect options to eradicate thrips.

Whitefly

Whitefly is a small, soft-bodied white fly, related to aphids, that lays eggs on the undersides of leaves. Whereas the adults are easy to see, the larvae are nearly impossible to spot and are actually what create the most damage on the plant by sucking its juices. Whiteflies congregate in groups and fly off the plant when the plant is moved.

Treatment: Take the plant outside and hose down the leaves until all whiteflies are removed. Spray the plant with insecticidal soap or a mixture of warm water and dish soap. Another option would be to use yellow sticky traps to capture adult whiteflies. Beneficial insects include green lacewings and ladybug larvae.

METHODS OF PEST REMOVAL: BENEFICIAL INSECTS, CHEMICAL, OR ORGANIC

Your method of pest control comes down to personal preference. IPM (integrated pest management), chemical insecticides, and organic insecticides are all effective in removing houseplant pests. Some approaches, like chemical insecticides, might yield faster results, but all have been proven effective in the long term.

Introducing chemicals to your home is always a risk, especially if children or animals are around, but as long as you keep them out of reach and closely follow the instructions on the label, you shouldn't experience problems and will see fast results.

Using organic products gives you the peace of mind that nothing you are using will be harmful to you, your pet, or your children. Organic products are safer to work with, but you might not see immediate or quick results. Homemade products are inexpensive and very effective.

IPM is a pest control technique that involves bringing in predatorial insects such as ladybugs or green lacewings to feed on the bad insects. As a result, seeing one of these beneficial insects flying around your house isn't uncommon. If living with these insects sounds unappealing, try the other options. Another option is to purchase these beneficial insects in larval form so they don't fly around your home.

COMMON HOUSEPLANT DISEASES

Bacterial Leaf Spots

Bacterial leaf spots are brown spots that appear on the leaves of houseplants. They sometimes have a yellow rim but are different than brown tips. Finding a bacterial leaf spot doesn't always mean the leaf will die, but will in some cases. These spots are caused by microscopic single-cell organisms and cool, wet conditions. Bacterial leaf spots spread quickly in the right conditions, so best to treat them as soon as you see them. Bacterial leaf spots are common for Anthurium plants, but any plant is susceptible to such spots.

Treatment: Applying copper fungicide is a great way to remove the bacteria that causes bacterial leaf spots, as is removing the leaf altogether to prevent the spread to other leaves and plants.

Brown Edges

Brown edges, brown tips, wilting leaves, and curling edges are some of the most common houseplant problems, especially with plants like Dracaena or Spider Plants. Brown edges and tips are signs of underwatering or an indication that the plant is putting energy into new growth. If your plant has brown edges but is still producing new growth, rest assured the plant is simply diverting energy. The type of water used can also cause brown tips. Extra minerals and salts in tap water can burn the leaves at the edges. Certain plants, like Calathea, are more sensitive to these minerals and salts and would prefer to be watered with rainwater or distilled water if you notice brown tips.

Treatment: Brown edges don't necessarily have a treatment, because once they begin to brown, that part of the leaf is dead. For aesthetic purposes, trim off the brown parts of your plant using sterilized scissors.

Curling Leaves

Curling edges are often caused by the plant being thirsty, or not having enough ambient humidity, or may be a symptom of pest damage.

Treatment: To help a plant with curling leaves, start by giving it water. If the plant has been watered and is still curling, check for a pest. If there is no pest, try providing more humidity for the plant.

Mold

Mold on the topsoil is a common occurrence on houseplants with poor soil aeration or drainage, or poor air flow in their room. Long periods of cloudy days can also prevent the soil from drying out as normal. White mold will grow on soil that stays too wet for too long, or on terra-cotta pots that have taken too long to dry out. This kind of mold is not harmful to humans or pets but is a sign of a soil or watering issue.

Treatment: If you find mold for the first time on the topsoil and the plant is showing no other signs of distress, sprinkle with ground cinnamon. Ground cinnamon contains cinnamaldehyde, an excellent natural anti-fungal treatment that will kill fungus spores in the soil. For recurring mold on your topsoil, remove as much soil from the plant as possible, and replace with new, better-draining soil. Be conscious of your watering and make sure your plant is allowed to dry out more between waterings. Throw away old soil.

Powdery Mildew

Powdery mildew is a fungal disease that, as the name suggests, produces powdery patches of white on the leaves and stems of all kinds of plants, including houseplants. Powdery mildew prevents the plant from photosynthesizing, which causes leaves to drop prematurely. Spores transfer from plant to plant, and with the right amount of moisture, germinate. Powdery mildew is especially common in Begonias.

Treatment: Create a mixture of 1 part neem oil, 1 squirt dish soap, 1 tablespoon baking soda, and 3 parts water. Shake the mixture before each use, and spray thoroughly over the leaves. Check on the plant each day to track its progress and keep spraying until the mildew is gone.

Root Rot

Root rot is caused when roots are not able to dry out and breathe or when a plant is severely underwatered and the roots shrink and end up rotting because they are unable to absorb moisture. Root rot most commonly looks like dark, mushy, sometimes smelly roots. These roots are easy to pull off and will sometimes leave behind a skinny root that resembles hair. Not all dark roots are rotted—some plants simply have darker roots. Roots are normally firm, so if you notice dark, mushy roots, you have root rot. Root rot occurs inside the pot in an area you wouldn't look often, but the leaves will show you signs. When a plant is experiencing root rot, the leaves will droop, even after watering, and will start to yellow and fall off. Sometimes, you might even find mold on the topsoil.

Treatment: To treat root rot, remove all old soil from the roots, as well as all rotted roots. Dead roots will not come back to life, but in the correct conditions, new roots will sprout. If the plant still has a substantial root system after removing the rot, repot into a better-draining soil mixture that gives the roots more air to breathe. If the root system is mostly depleted, place the plant in water to help the roots rehabilitate and grow. Add a small amount of liquid fertilizer in with the water to give the plant nutrients to grow.

Wilting Leaves

Wilting leaves are almost always a sign the plant is thirsty. Many plants are visually vocal when thirsty, and wilting is one way to easily tell a plant needs water. Some plants will dramatically droop to the point of looking dead but will perk right back up after a good watering. Another reason leaves might wilt is if they are getting too much light or are experiencing root rot.

Treatment: If the plant is wilting and has dry soil, give your plant a drink! Your plant is communicating thirst. If the plant is wilting a few hours after being watered, and you watered when the soil was still moist, remove the plant from the pot and check if the roots are rotted. If you find mushy, brown roots, the plant has developed root rot. Remove all mushy roots, and if the root system is big enough, repot into a better-draining soil mixture that contains higher amounts of coco chips, pumice, or perlite. If the root system is severely damaged, place the plant in water so the roots can regrow. Repot when the roots are several inches long.

Viruses

Viruses are the most serious of houseplant ailments and should be treated. Mosaic viruses, spread by insects, are most common. How these viruses show up really depends on the plant, but, generally, symptoms include abnormal mottled coloring and stunted or deformed growth. To prevent these viruses, perform preventive pest management. When you discover mosaic viruses, check surrounding plants to make sure they are not infected and sterilize your plant tools with rubbing alcohol between uses to prevent the spread of disease.

Treatment: Because no treatment exists for mosaic viruses, the infected plant is best disposed of.

KEEPING PETS AWAY FROM PLANTS

Many houseplants are toxic to pets. These tips can help keep pets and plants safe:

- Move any toxic plants to a hard-to-reach place for pets, whether putting them on stands or in a room where pets aren't allowed.
- Provide an alternative for pets to chew on or play with—maybe a bone or chew toy for dogs, and for cats, perhaps their very own patch of cat grass. Cat grass is easily grown from seed, and the many health benefits make this plant an attractive solution.
- Tell pets no when they approach your houseplants. Provide positive reinforcement so they know backing away was the right thing to do.
- Spray plants with citrus or bitter apple to deter pets from ingesting them.

If your pet has ingested a toxic plant, call your veterinarian. Some symptoms include vomiting, diarrhea, and difficulty breathing. Even if a plant isn't technically toxic, minor symptoms like an upset stomach are not uncommon.

CONCLUSION

Remember that your houseplants will experience pests or disease (or both) at some point. These problems are not a negative reflection on you. Being able to identify problems with your houseplants will propel you to find solutions and widen your knowledge. Some plants are more susceptible to certain pests and disease, and the more time you spend with them, the more quickly you'll spot emerging problems.

Spend time inspecting your plants and perform preventative maintenance to avoid large and overwhelming outbreaks. Each time you water a plant, check the undersides of the leaves and along the petioles just to make sure nothing has moved in since you last checked. The best way to win the fight against pests and disease is to catch the problem early before anything has spread to more plants.

Houseplant pests and diseases have a tendency to scare new plant parents, but when addressed properly, are almost always simple to eliminate. By utilizing the techniques in this chapter, you'll be able to identify and eradicate the pests and diseases that seek to harm your plants. Over time, you'll notice similar symptoms among your plants and be able to identify problems quickly. Experience is the best gift to give yourself as a plant parent, so dig into each experience and learn as much as you can.

Chapter 5

HELP! COMMON HOUSEPLANT SCENARIOS

Most houseplants experience many of the same ailments. Learning to analyze the symptoms will help you understand what exactly is going wrong with your plant and find the solution. Feeling fearful or nervous about your plants when they display even the slightest signs of distress is common and okay—just take a step back to see what's really going on. Remember that houseplants are living things, and they won't always have perfect green leaves. Your early houseplants might have extensive evidence of your practicing and learning, and that's fine. Let's take a look at some common houseplant problems.

My plant looks unwell after I repotted it in a bigger container. What did I do wrong?

Plants commonly experience shock after a change of environment or when you bring them home from the nursery. If your plant is looking droopy and sad after repotting, the likely culprit is needing to adjust to their new home. Some plants are sensitive to disturbing their roots and take a little extra time to feel safe in their new environment. As long as you have helped the plant settle in by watering it well after repotting, expect it to perk up within the next couple of days. If after a few days the plant still looks droopy and sad, check the roots to make sure they aren't rotting.

I think I overwatered my Fiddle-Leaf Fig. The plant is suddenly droopy and the leaves look very dull.

A droopy plant has a few possibilities. First, check for pests that feed on the juices of plants and leave the leaves looking dull, curly, and sometimes droopy. If you know you haven't watered the plant in a while and the soil is completely dried out, droopy leaves are a sign of thirst. If the plant is not thirsty, doesn't have a pest, and is still droopy and dull, the plant could be experiencing root rot. Unpot the plant to take a look at the roots and check how viable they are. If the roots are dark and mushy, or thin and stringy, the roots are rotted and need to be removed.

My Aloe Vera plant is dry and browning on the ends.

Aloe Vera plants will sometimes brown their leaf edges when they are not receiving enough water. Even though they are considered drought tolerant, they do still need to be watered. Desert plants can live up to a few weeks without showing signs of thirst, but when you do water, water the plant deeply to best simulate their natural environment. Though the brown tips aren't the best aesthetically, they're proof that you are learning. New growth will come in free of brown tips, and eventually you can remove the older leaves.

My plant is getting yellow leaves though I have watered correctly and am providing the right sunlight.

Yellow leaves aren't always a sign your plant is sick or needs some-thing. The location of the yellow leaves is what is important to consider. Newer growth turning yellow signals an unhealthy plant and is telling you there's a problem. Check for pests and let the plant dry out a little more between waterings. Yellowing older growth could be a sign of underwatering. A plant in distress from thirst will kill off the oldest leaves to ensure continued growth. If you are watering correctly but find an occasional yellow leaf that is older growth, rest assured know-ing the plant is just making room and diverting energy to new growth. After all, leaves aren't meant to stick around forever.

My plant's leaves are turning brown and crispy before they even unfurl.

A leaf dying before unfurling, or opening, is typically a sign of under-watering. A plant not receiving the proper watering will kill off new growth to maintain current growth. To prevent this situation from happening, look out for signs of thirst or stick your finger in the soil to check moisture levels. If the soil is dry about two knuckles down, the plant is probably ready for a watering.

The plant has put out big growth before but is suddenly putting out smaller and smaller leaves.

Typically, small growth is a sign of not enough light, though other culprits could be at play. Plants will revert back to producing juvenile leaves when they don't have the proper tools to continue growing bigger. Check the light and check the roots. Place your plant in a spot with brighter light and consider pruning off the small and stringy growth. Pruning your plant encourages bushier tendencies and will eventually result in a fuller plant.

I moved my plant to a place I thought would be better, but I'm finding dropped leaves.

Many houseplants, especially Ficus, do not like to be moved around. In nature, plants are not able to get up and move to a different location, so when they find their spot, they stay there. You'll want to treat the plants in your home in a similar way. Moving plants throughout your home will likely provide different lighting, air flow, and temperature. With these kinds of changes, they drop leaves, especially when you first bring them home. The plant will regrow leaves and fill back out once reacclimated.

My plant hasn't put out any new growth even in the growing season.

Your plant's soil can be depleted of its nutrients after a few months. If you don't replace the nutrients by fertilizing, your plant will either not grow or produce stunted growth. Choose a fertilizer you like best and keep up with a regular fertilizing schedule to ensure your plant continues to grow at a healthy rate. Another possibility is that the plant is root-bound, which tends to halt growth. As soon as your plant has more room to grow, it will start putting out new growth again.

My cactus is suddenly very soft and squishy. Is my plant dying? Is there anything I can do?

A cactus is dead once it becomes soft and squishy. Cacti and succulents are accustomed to long periods of drought; if you water too often and don't allow the soil to dry out, the plant will rot. This kind of rot cannot be reversed, although stopping the progression is possible if you notice what's happening in time and are able to stop it. The difference between an overwatered and underwatered cactus is the presence or absence of wrinkles. An underwatered cactus will get wrinkly and easily bendable, but the shape of an overwatered cactus remains intact but is squishy to the touch. With cacti, it's better to remain on the side of underwatering because hydrating is easier than dehydrating.

I put my plant in a bright window to provide more sun. Now black spots are all over the plant and the leaves are drooping.

The sudden appearance of black or brown spots after moving a plant into more light is sunburn. Our houseplants have incredibly tender foliage not meant for full sun. Some plants will experience sunburn even indoors because the light is so intense or the leaves are so tender, or both. A sunburned plant, while an eyesore, is not dead. New leaves will grow in and replace old, damaged ones. To avoid sunburn on your houseplants, place a sheer white curtain in front of your windows to diffuse the light. Also, since plants live most of their lives in the same conditions, suddenly throwing them into much higher light than they're used to is bound to end badly. If you would like to move a plant to fuller sun, slowly move the plant closer and closer to the window, or leave in the sun for only a few minutes at a time. Increase the time in the sun each day, but do so extremely slowly. Plants need time to acclimate to high amounts of sunlight.

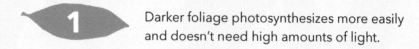

As you begin your houseplant adventure, here are 12 general tips to keep in mind:

1 Darker foliage photosynthesizes more easily and doesn't need high amounts of light.

2 Remember, low light does not mean no light. If you can't comfortably read a book in a room lit by natural light, there isn't enough light for a plant to grow.

3 How often you water depends in part on lighting—a plant in brighter light uses more energy and the soil dries more quickly, thus needing more water.

4 Cacti and succulents tend to have small, shallow root systems and require smaller pots to allow the soil to dry more quickly.

5 Thick, waxy leaves indicate a plant holds on to water longer than thin-leaf plants.

6 **Variegation** and colors are made bolder by brighter light—just keep in mind the brightness limitations of the specific plant.

7 Plants generally don't like sudden temperature changes or being moved around. If you must move the plant, try to do so very gradually, a few feet at a time.

8 When some plants receive an abundance of light, their leaves may turn a pinkish color, an indication of sun stress. This condition may sound bad, but it means that the plant is getting a lot of light. The situation should be monitored, but rest assured the plant is not in distress.

9 Propagate most cacti by cutting off an appendage, letting it callous over for 1 to 2 days, and planting it in soil.

10 Deadheading a plant can spark new ways for a plant to grow. Some plants, like those in the Ficus **genus**, will branch out when you cut off the top. Try placing the cut piece in water and waiting for roots to replant later.

11 Most plants, aside from cacti, benefit from regular fertilizer during growing season.

12 When cut, the Euphorbia produces a highly toxic, white milky sap. Wash your hands thoroughly if this sticky substance gets on you.

PART TWO

PLANT PROFILES

Now that you have learned how to care for your plants, let's talk about the plants that you could call your own. Here you'll find profiles of the most popular houseplants, grouped from low to high maintenance. Each profile indicates the likely size of the plant when you find it in a garden center, the plant's growth habit, its typical cost, and its pet friendliness. Get to know the plants throughout these pages and practice your plant identification skills the next time you head out to the garden center!

Chapter 6

LOW-MAINTENANCE PLANTS

AFRICAN VIOLET
Saintpaulia ionantha

Size: Up to 8 inches tall   **Growth Habit:** Bushy, Upright   **Cost Rating:** $

PET FRIENDLY

African Violets are best known for their colorful flowers that emerge from thick, fuzzy, round leaves. They come in many varieties, some with variegated (discrete markings of different colors) leaves, and flowers ranging from white to deep purple to pink.

Care: African Violets have very sensitive foliage and can suffer from leaf burn if water sits on their leaves. Carefully water your African Violet by pulling up the foliage and watering underneath. Bottom watering your African Violet is another option, but even so, occasionally water it from the top (under the leaves) to flush out excess minerals. Although needing sufficient drainage, this plant does enjoy more water retention, so use a mixture a bit heavier in coco peat. Blooms last a number of months, but once they die off, more will come in. For light, place your African Violet pulled back from bright windows, away from direct sun.

Tip: African Violets easily propagate by cutting off a leaf and placing it into soil or other propagation mediums. Soon you will see a new crown of leaves forming.

ALOE VERA
Aloe barbadensis

Size: Up to 2+ feet tall   **Growth Habit:** Upright   **Cost Rating:** $

NOT PET FRIENDLY

Although not all Aloe is medicinal, the Aloe Vera plant is. Aloe Vera is known particularly for its healing properties for the skin, so the next time you get sunburned, reach for the Aloe Vera. This plant has long, thick arms and a light green, sometimes blueish, hue. As extremely prolific growers, Aloe Vera plants are satisfying houseplants.

Care: Like other desert plants, Aloe Vera plants enjoy lots of light and would be perfectly happy living in or near a bright south-facing window indoors. Succulent leaves hold water, making the plant extremely drought resistant. For soil, provide an extremely chunky mixture that drains through immediately, like that used for cactus. Use additives that hold moisture, like pumice and coco chips, but do not keep the soil saturated.

> **Tip:** To use your Aloe medicinally, cut off the arm close to the base of the plant and slice open. The thick, goopy liquid inside the leaf soothes burns of all kinds and has other benefits. An Aloe leaf will keep in a cup of water on the counter for up to 2 weeks.

ALUMINUM PLANT/WATERMELON PILEA
Pilea cadierei

Size: Up to 1+ feet tall   **Growth Habit:** Upright   **Cost Rating:** $

NOT PET FRIENDLY

The Aluminum Plant has oval leaves with pointed ends that feature silver ripples in parallel lines along the leaf. This understory plant, native to China, grows at the bottom of the rainforest floor.

Care: The Aluminum Plant is notable for its ability to thrive in low light. Place this plant in darker spaces, but not places without any sun exposure. Pulled back from most windows will be sufficient. The plant is happy to dry out between waterings and will droop when thirsty. For soil, the Aluminum Plant enjoys a moisture-holding mixture a bit heavier on coco peat that includes other additives, like perlite, to help drainage. Fertilizing every couple of weeks will make this plant happy.

Did You Know: The Aluminum Plant is related to nettle.

ANGEL-WING BEGONIA
Begonia lucerna

Size: Up to 1+ feet tall   **Growth Habit:** Upright   **Cost Rating:** $

NOT PET FRIENDLY

The Angel-Wing Begonia hybrid comes from Lucerne, Switzerland. Long, dark green leaves with bright red undersides and silver polka dots on the fronts of the leaves identify this plant.

Care: The Angel-Wing Begonia enjoys bright light and can handle small amounts of direct sun. Place in an east-facing window or pulled back from a west-facing one. Water when you notice the soil is about three-quarters dried out, or when the plant visibly droops toward the floor and the leaves feel thinner. The soil mixture should be well-draining, but slightly more coco-peat-based to help the plant retain moisture while still giving the roots room to breathe.

Tip: As a cane Begonia, this plant will likely need a stake to stay upright once larger.

ARECA PALM/BUTTERFLY PALM/CANE PALM
Dypsis lutescens

Size: Up to 2 feet tall   **Growth Habit:** Upright   **Cost Rating:** $

PET FRIENDLY

The Areca Palm is commonly used as a houseplant and in landscaping in sub-tropical and tropical areas. This palm has long stems with delicate palm fronds at the end of each.

Care: The Areca Palm needs high light, so it does best near south- or west-facing windows. While not needing direct light for multiple hours, this plant enjoys as much sun as possible without developing a sunburn. Plant in a chunky soil mixture that allows water to drain out quickly. Water when you see the soil is about half dry.

Tip: This palm is more sensitive to fluoride in water, so if you see brown tips on your palm, this relatively normal reaction may be the reason.

BABY RUBBER PLANT/AMERICAN RUBBER PLANT
Peperomia obtusifolia

Size: Up to 1+ feet tall **Growth Habit:** Upright **Cost Rating:** $

PET FRIENDLY

One of the most popular Peperomia houseplants, the *Peperomia obtusifolia*, commonly known as the Baby Rubber Plant, American Rubber Plant, or Pepper Face Plant, comes in a variegated form and a solid green form. The leaves are small, oval, and waxy. Their similarity to succulents makes them wonderful houseplants for beginners.

Care: This plant does not need direct light but will thrive in bright indirect light. Place near an east- or west-facing window or pulled slightly back from a south-facing window. The water reservoir in the leaves and stems means the Baby Rubber Plant does not need to be watered often; instead, water when the leaves are pliable and soft. The soil mixture should be light and airy, and water should always drain quickly out of the bottom of the pot. You only need to fertilize this plant a few times during the growing season.

Did You Know: This plant as the name suggests–Baby Rubber Plant–resembles the Rubber Plant (*Ficus elastica*, page 164), only smaller. However, this one is much easier to care for.

BASEBALL PLANT
Euphorbia obesa

Size: Up to 4 inches tall   **Growth Habit:** Mound, Upright   **Cost Rating:** $$

NOT PET FRIENDLY

The Baseball Plant is a unique member of the Euphorbia genus native to parts of South Africa. Typically sold as a singular small, round plant, it eventually stretches out and grows tall.

Care: The Baseball Plant enjoys bright light from a south-facing window or full sun outdoors. Use a well-draining, chunky soil mixture to allow water to drain quickly, while maintaining pockets of moisture. Use coco chips as your base and add in pumice and a small amount of compost. Water every 2 to 3 weeks, or when the soil is completely dried out. This plant will become soft and mushy and will die if overwatered.

Tip: Plants in the Euphorbia genus produce a highly toxic white milky sap. Wash your hands thoroughly if this substance gets on your skin.

BISHOP'S CAP CACTUS/BISHOP'S MITER
Astrophytum myriostigma

Size: Up to 4 inches tall   **Growth Habit:** Upright   **Cost Rating:** $

PET FRIENDLY BUT IRRITATING

The name "Bishop's Cap" Cactus comes from the plant's strong resemblance to a bishop's headgear. The collection of cacti in the Astrophytum genus grow as one large, round piece.

Care: This cactus needs full sun for at least a few hours a day and is well suited for being outside or on a south-facing windowsill. The body is like a large water tank that stays filled for many months. Avoid watering the plant in the wintertime, but water about once a month during the summer months. Astrophytum, and most cacti, have a notably small root system, so plant the cactus in an extremely well-draining soil mixture, made up largely of coco chips and pumice and small amounts of compost. Be sure to account for the small root system when choosing your pot.

Tip: While not toxic to pets, this cactus will irritate your pet's stomach if ingested.

BLUE CANDLE
Myrtillocactus geometrizans

Size: Up to 1 foot tall   **Growth Habit:** Upright   **Cost Rating:** $

PET FRIENDLY BUT IRRITATING

The *Myrtillocactus geometrizans*, or Blue Candle, is an upright cactus best known for its blue hue. The powdery substance that is responsible for this blue is called glaucous and serves as a natural sunscreen and barrier from bacteria or disease.

Care: The Blue Candle needs full sun so is best suited for a south-facing window if grown indoors. Water every 3 or 4 weeks, as this plant is very drought tolerant. Plant in a well-draining soil mixture that allows water to drain immediately. Cacti do not like to sit in moisture for too long because they use their succulent trunks to store moisture. Fertilize at the beginning and end of the growing season.

Tip: While not toxic to pets, this cactus will irritate
your pet's stomach if ingested.

BOSTON FERN
Nephrolepis exaltata

Size: Up to 2 feet tall   **Growth Habit:** Bushy, Upright   **Cost Rating:** $

PET FRIENDLY

The Boston Fern is commonly grown inside and on covered patios outside. Like other ferns, this one has bushy growth with countless fronds growing from the center of the plant. There is a classic green version, but you might be able to find one that's variegated, called the Boston Tiger Fern.

Care: Though Boston Ferns are hardy, they still require a lot of the same care as other ferns. To keep the plant as happy as possible, place it in high humidity, above 50 percent, and in a cool, shaded place. If outside, keep on a completely covered patio. Inside, pull back from all windows. Make sure your soil mixture is good for moisture retention while still well-draining. For best results, plant your Boston Fern in a plastic or ceramic pot.

Did You Know: Ferns are some of the oldest plants known to humans, dating back 360 million years!

BUNNY EAR CACTUS/POLKA-DOT CACTUS
Opuntia microdasys

Size: Up to 1 foot tall   **Growth Habit:** Upright   **Cost Rating:** $

NOT PET FRIENDLY

The Bunny Ear Cactus is a well-known and widely accessible cactus variety with a fuzzy appearance. These "fuzzy" parts are actually not fuzzy but are clusters of tiny spines that fall off easily and attach into fingers or whatever else brushes up against them. The cactus grows in a segmented form, stacking new pads on top of one another.

Care: This plant enjoys high amounts of light. If indoors, place in a south-facing window. Water sparingly, only about once a month, and even less frequently in winter. Plant your cactus in a chunky and well-draining soil mixture containing small amounts of compost and peat in comparison to other soil mixtures.

Tip: To propagate, simply cut off a pad, let it callous over for 24 hours, and plant it in a cactus soil mixture. The plant will soon put out roots, and eventually, new growth.

BURLE MARX PHILODENDRON
Philodendron imbe

Size: Up to 3 feet tall   **Growth Habit:** Upright   **Cost Rating:** $$

NOT PET FRIENDLY

The Burle Marx Philodendron is a narrow, heart-shaped-leaf plant with glossy, dark green leaves. Native to Brazil, this plant can be found climbing up trees and growing large leaves.

Care: The Burle Marx Philodendron prefers bright light, but no direct sun, such as near an east- or west-facing window or under dappled light from a south-facing exposure. Water the Burle Marx Philodendron when the soil is almost completely dried out. The thick leaves and stems help hold water, but the plant shouldn't dry out for too long. Use a well-draining, chunky soil mixture. Like most epiphytes, this plant enjoys climbing; a fun way to foster this tendency in your home is to use a moss pole or stake.

Did You Know: Burle Marx plants—pronounced "bur-lee marks"—are named after Roberto Burle Marx, a Brazilian landscape architect, painter, ecologist, and naturalist who used native plants as a part of his landscape designs.

CHINESE EVERGREEN/PHILIPPINE EVERGREEN
Aglaonema commutatum

Size: Up to 2+ feet tall   **Growth Habit:** Bushy, Upright   **Cost Rating:** $

NOT PET FRIENDLY

Though Chinese Evergreens come in many different leaf shapes and colors, they are all simple to care for. This plant requires very little from you, and provides consistent, beautiful, bushy growth in return—a cute addition to any houseplant collection.

Care: The Chinese Evergreen is a great plant for low-light spaces. With minimal needs, the plant is a happy grower no matter the conditions. Use a well-draining soil mixture. The plant will get droopy when thirsty, so water when the soil is almost or completely dried out. As a plant that thrives on neglect, the Chinese Evergreen is best left alone.

Tip: As the plant matures, older growth will turn yellow and die off. If the lower stem is beginning to look bare, cut the stem about 4 inches below the leaves, and place in water to grow a new root system. Replant in soil once the roots have matured.

CORN PLANT/CORNSTALK DRACAENA/FALSE PALM
Dracaena fragrans

Size: Up to 4+ feet   **Growth Habit:** Upright   **Cost Rating:** $

NOT PET FRIENDLY

The Corn Plant is a larger member of the Asparagaceae plant family. Usually already multiple feet tall when you find them for sale in plant stores and nurseries, they are aptly named because their growth habit resembles that of corn. They feature a long stalk with long, pointed foliage bursting out of the top, the latter of which has a lighter green stripe down the middle.

Care: Caring for the Corn Plant is simple. Able to handle low-light situations, it should be placed in a northern exposure or pulled far back from east-, west-, or south-facing windows. If you have a darker corner, this plant is the likely choice for that space. Low light doesn't mean no light, however. The amount of light this plant (and all plants) gets will affect how often you need to water, because plants absorb moisture in ratio to how much light they receive. This plant likes to dry out almost completely between waterings, so plant in a well-draining, chunky soil mixture.

Did You Know: Dracaena comes from the Greek word *drakaina*, which means "female dragon."

CREEPING CHARLIE/GROUND IVY
Glechoma hederacea

Size: Up to 3+ feet tall   **Growth Habit:** Crawling, Trailing   **Cost Rating:** $

NOT PET FRIENDLY

The Creeping Charlie is an extremely prolific, even invasive, plant native to parts of Europe. The plant was first introduced to North America as groundcover.

Care: Creeping Charlie is not accustomed to receiving direct sunlight and will do best pulled back from bright windows. Your soil mixture should be well-draining and chunky. The plant likes to remain moist and doesn't take well to being dried out for too long; otherwise, you might see leaves begin to fall off. Not to worry, though—if you run into these troubles with your Creeping Charlie, rest assured knowing that the leaves will soon be replaced because the plant grows quickly.

CROWN OF THORNS/CHRIST PLANT

Euphorbia milii

Size: Up to 2+ feet tall   **Growth Habit:** Upright   **Cost Rating:** $

NOT PET FRIENDLY

The Crown of Thorns is a flowering Euphorbia native to Madagascar. Known for branches that yield a multitude of thorns, they also have small, round green leaves and colorful bracts (modified leaf or scale with a flower cluster). They can come in a variety of colors, from yellow to pink to red.

Care: This prolific grower benefits from high amounts of light in a south-facing window or outside on a shaded patio. Like its Euphorbia counterparts, the Crown of Thorns is not a cactus but can be treated similarly. Use a chunky, succulent soil mixture heavy in additives like coco chips and pumice. Water sparingly to ensure a healthy plant. The Crown of Thorns always seems to be in bloom, thanks to colorful bracts. Be careful when trimming or cutting any type of Euphorbia because of the extremely poisonous white sap harmful to the eyes, mouth, or skin. If you do touch this sticky substance, wash immediately.

Did You Know: Bracts attract pollinators.

DONKEY'S TAIL
Sedum morganianum

Size: Up to 2+ feet long   **Growth Habit:** Trailing   **Cost Rating:** $

NOT PET FRIENDLY

Donkey's Tail is a **trailing** succulent native to southern Mexico with small, delicate, light green leaves that have a tail-like appearance with long cascading branches.

Care: Be gentle with Donkey's Tail leaves and branches. The leaves are extremely delicate and can fall off at the slightest disturbance. The good news is they are easy to propagate if they do fall off. Provide your plant with as much light as the indoors will provide, for instance, by placing it in or near a south- or west-facing window. If you have space on your patio, they will enjoy the bright light there, too. The Donkey's Tail will get wrinkly when thirsty, but it only needs to be watered about once a month. These factors depend on how much light the plant is receiving, which, in turn, determines how much energy the plant is using.

Did You Know: Succulents have shallow root systems, best planted in an equally shallow pot. If there is significantly more soil than roots in the pot, you run the risk of rot because the soil will hold moisture for too long. You might be surprised by how small succulent root systems are, so always choose your pot based on root size, not necessarily the size of the foliage.

ECHEVERIA
Echeveria elegans

Size: Up to 1 foot tall   **Growth Habit:** Upright   **Cost Rating:** $

NOT PET FRIENDLY

Echeveria is a genus of succulents native to Mexico, South America, and Central America. These plants are often characterized by their rosette shape and variety of colors from plant to plant. The thick leaves are usually covered with a white powder called epicuticular wax that protects them from moisture loss and sunburn.

Care: Echeveria generally benefits from high-light environments, doing best in south- or west-facing windows or on your patio. If receiving an abundance of light, the leaves may turn pinkish with sun stress, which is not inherently bad for the plant. If not receiving enough light, the plant will begin to stretch out. Water well about once a month for the moisture to fully penetrate the soil. Wrinkly leaves will let you know if the plant gets thirsty before you water. Go with very chunky soil that allows water to drain through quickly to avoid rot.

Tip: To propagate Echeveria, pull off leaves (or take fallen leaves) and place them on top of a tray or shallow pot of soil. Keep the topsoil moist by misting in the mornings, and watch as the leaves grow roots, and eventually a whole new plant.

ENGLISH IVY/COMMON IVY
Hedera helix

Size: Up to 4+ feet tall   **Growth Habit:** Climbing, Trailing   **Cost Rating:** $

NOT PET FRIENDLY

English Ivy is a popular choice. A prolific grower, this houseplant can also climb or trail and comes in both dark green and variegated varieties. English Ivy is native to multiple regions throughout Europe and has an easy nature.

Care: English Ivy doesn't need tons of light, but to determine proper lighting, consider the coloring on the leaves. Dark green English Ivy will require less light than the higher light required for variegated varieties. Either way, this plant will send out long stems and branches and latch onto anything around. Allow to dry out at least 1 to 2 inches down between waterings. English Ivy likes a well-draining mixture that allows water to run out of the drainage holes immediately. A bit more moisture retention may help, because some of these plants can be very thirsty. This plant needs a lot of nutrients because it is a prolific grower, so fertilize about every 2 weeks during the growing season.

FEATHER CACTUS
Mammillaria plumosa

Size: Up to 6 inches tall   **Growth Habit:** Mound   **Cost Rating:** $$

NOT PET FRIENDLY

The Feather Cactus's name comes from soft, feather-like spines, which appear sharp but are surprisingly not. The plant grows in low, dense mounds that often look like clumps of cotton balls.

Care: The Feather Cactus needs high amounts of light and, when grown indoors, is best suited for south-facing windows. When you water this plant, make sure water doesn't sit on the spines for too long. In the plant's native environment, water evaporates quickly, but it may not in your home. For soil, use a well-draining and chunky soil mixture, which could include coco chips, pumice, and small amounts of compost.

GASTERIA BRACHYPHYLLA

Gasteria brachyphylla

Size: Up to 4 inches tall   **Growth Habit:** Upright   **Cost Rating:** $

NOT PET FRIENDLY

Native to the Western Cape of South Africa, the *Gasteria brachyphylla* is a succulent with long, flat leaves that grow left or right from the center of the plant. The leaves are often dark green with lighter green spots or stripes.

Care: *Gasteria brachyphylla* is one of the only succulents that can handle a bit of lower light. Don't interpret this to mean that the Gasteria Brachyphylla is a low-light plant, but feel free to provide the priority seating in your south-facing window to another plant. Water when the soil is completely dried out, and choose a chunky, well-draining soil. Use an organic fertilizer at the beginning and end of the growing season.

GOLDEN POTHOS
Epipremnum aureum

Size: Up to 5+ feet long   **Growth Habit:** Climbing, Trailing   **Cost Rating:** $

NOT PET FRIENDLY

The Golden Pothos is a tried-and-true classic houseplant you probably grew up seeing everywhere. Commonly grown in water or soil and cascading down shelves, this plant also loves to climb up a trellis or moss pole. This variety is special because of the gold and yellow flecks of variegation on each leaf.

Care: The Golden Pothos is happy to live wherever suits you best, as long as the plant has access to some kind of light. A common choice for offices, this plant can even happily grow under artificial light, including fluorescent bulbs. Choose a well-draining, chunky soil, and allow the plant to dry out completely between waterings. When thirsty, the Golden Pothos will droop and the leaves will become soft and thin.

Tip: If you'd like to share your plant with friends, the Golden Pothos is very easy to propagate. Cut the stem just under a node, remove the bottom leaves, and submerge in water until roots form. Transplant to soil or leave in water!

GOLDFISH PLANT
Nematanthus nervosus

Size: Up to 2 feet long   **Growth Habit:** Hanging   **Cost Rating:** $

PET FRIENDLY

The Goldfish Plant's name comes from the flowers that strongly resemble goldfish. This plant is a prolific bloomer and has leaves that are small, dark green, waxy, and shiny.

Care: Being darker-leaved, this plant doesn't need high light, but it would do well in the bright indirect light provided by pulling the plant a foot or two away from windows where sun rays do not directly fall upon the leaves. Water your Goldfish Plant when you notice the soil is almost completely dried out. If you wait too long between waterings, you will notice leaves falling off. A well-draining soil mixture is a must.

Tip: The Goldfish Plant is easy to propagate by cutting a stem, pulling off about 3 inches of lower leaves, and placing it in water, or directly into soil with rooting hormone.

HEARTLEAF PHILODENDRON
Philodendron cordatum

Size: Up to 2+ feet tall   **Growth Habit:** Climbing, Trailing   **Cost Rating:** $

NOT PET FRIENDLY

The Heartleaf Philodendron is a simple-to-care-for houseplant. Best known for heart-shaped leaves and wonderful deep green foliage, this plant can be trained to grow across a bookshelf or wall, or up a trellis to produce bigger leaves.

Care: The Heartleaf Philodendron is a simple plant with simple needs and can survive in low-light situations. Depending on proximity to the window, this plant will be happy in a north-, south-, east-, or west-facing window. Use a well-draining soil, especially in a lower-light situation. If the plant becomes leggy or the leaves are getting progressively smaller, don't be afraid to prune and propagate what you've cut off. Cut below a node and submerge in water until the roots grow a few inches long. The Heartleaf Philodendron will get soft and curly when thirsty, a sign to water deeply.

HOLIDAY CACTUS
(CHRISTMAS, EASTER, THANKSGIVING)
Schlumbergera (general)

Size: Up to 1+ feet long   **Growth Habit:** Trailing   **Cost Rating:** $

PET FRIENDLY BUT IRRITATING

There are several types of Holiday Cactus that are really jungle cactus with slightly variant leaf shapes. They grow in a segmented form. Christmas Cactus (*Schlumbergera bridgesii*) has longer, more rectangular leaves; Thanksgiving Cactus (*Schlumbergera truncata*) has rectangular leaves with several pointed tips along the side edges; and Easter Cactus (*Hatiora gaertneri*) has ovate leaves. Their care is exactly the same.

Care: Holiday cacti can handle lower amounts of light, which means these plants would be happy pulled back from an east-, west-, or south-facing window, or sitting in a north-facing one. When exposed to high amounts of light, the segments will turn pink, and in extreme cases, yellow. Plant in a well-draining, chunky soil mixture to allow the roots to breathe properly. Water when the soil is almost completely dried out, and soak the soil deeply.

Tip: This plant will be triggered to bloom when daylight drops below 13 hours a day.

HOYA CARNOSA/WAX PLANT
Hoya carnosa

Size: Up to 3+ feet long   **Growth Habit:** Trailing   **Cost Rating:** $

PET FRIENDLY WITH EXCEPTIONS

The Hoya Carnosa is one of the most common Hoya varieties. Many popular Hoyas are mutated from this original and take on different leaf characteristics. The Wax Plant nickname of the Hoya Carnosa is due to the thick, shiny leaves that appear waxed. The simple nature and beauty of this plant make it widely loved. Choose from solid green or any of the variegated varieties.

Care: The easygoing Hoya Carnosa won't ask for much. Provide a chunky soil mixture and consider adding orchid bark. The leaves get thin and easily bendable when the plant is thirsty, but because the leaves serve as a water reservoir, you won't need to water often. Frequency of watering will depend on the size of the pot and proximity to the light source. This plant will thrive in bright light from an east- or west-facing window, or pulled back from a south-facing window. Higher humidity will usually result in more growth.

Tip: If your plant is seldom putting out new growth and has been in the same pot for a while, consider repotting into a slightly larger home.

HOYA KERRII/SWEETHEART HOYA
Hoya kerrii

Size: Up to 2 feet tall   **Growth Habit:** Trailing, Upright   **Cost Rating:** $$

NOT PET FRIENDLY

The Hoya Kerrii is a large-leaf, heart-shaped Hoya with green and variegated varieties. The variegation can either be on the margins of the leaves or the inside. Like other Hoya plants, the leaves on the Hoya Kerrii hold water, making the plant adaptable to drought conditions.

Care: The Hoya Kerrii can handle bright light: up to a few hours of cool direct sun. They are well suited for east-facing windows for this reason. You only need to water when the leaves start to soften and become pliable. Like most other Hoya plants, this one likes to live in soil that is well-draining and chunky, full of orchid bark and other soil additives like pumice. To give it a nutrient boost, use both **foliar** and soil fertilizer.

Did You Know: The Hoya Kerrii is often sold around Valentine's Day as single-heart plants (thus the Sweetheart nickname). Oftentimes, they are without a node, which is essential for the plant to continue to produce new leaves. If your Hoya Kerrii has a node under the soil, you will see a new branch form eventually.

HOYA KRIMSON PRINCESS
Hoya carnosa

Size: Up to 2 feet long   **Growth Habit:** Trailing   **Cost Rating:** $

NOT PET FRIENDLY

The Hoya Krimson Princess is a variation of the *Hoya carnosa* that features green, white, and sometimes pink variegation on the inside margins of the leaves. Pink will appear on new growth and might stick around depending on how sun-stressed the plant is.

Care: This plant needs high amounts of light and does best in an east- or west-facing window. These placements will encourage the plant to continue to put out highly variegated leaves. Water your Hoya Krimson Princess when the leaves become pliable, or when the soil is completely dried out. If you wait too long between waterings, you might find that older leaves yellow and die off. Plant this Hoya in a bark-heavy soil mixture that allows water to quickly drain out the bottom.

HOYA OBOVATA
Hoya obovata

Size: Up to 2 feet long   **Growth Habit:** Trailing   **Cost Rating:** $

NOT PET FRIENDLY

The large, circular leaves of the Hoya Obovata are striking. Most also feature silver speckling, which can turn pink under bright light situations. These plants are happy to trail and cascade but can also grow up a trellis nicely. This Hoya is typical with thick, waxy leaves, but under proper circumstances, a mature plant will produce a white flower with small pink features.

Care: For best results, plant your Obovata in a well-draining and chunky soil mixture to allow the roots to breathe properly. The Obovata can handle strong light from a south- or west-facing window—with strong light, the plant will likely produce quick growth. When the plant is thirsty, the leaves will become thin and pliable. Use a foliar spray or an organic fertilizer. The Hoya Obovata doesn't necessarily need high humidity, but the plant will benefit from 40 percent humidity or higher.

Did You Know: The Hoya Obovata will sometimes grow long runner stems—don't cut them off! Eventually, this stem will grow leaves or even a flower.

INCH PLANT

Tradescantia zebrina

Size: Up to 2+ feet long   **Growth Habit:** Trailing   **Cost Rating:** $

NOT PET FRIENDLY

The Inch Plant is native to Mexico and Central America and known for its purple leaves with silvery-green horizontal stripes. A quick and easy grower, this plant shouldn't give you any problems.

Care: The Inch Plant needs bright indirect light such as in an east- or west-facing window; otherwise, the silvery-green stripes will fade away. Allow your Inch Plant to dry out about halfway between waterings, but don't wait too long or the leaves close to the base of the plant will turn yellow and die. To prevent root rot, be sure the soil mixture is well-draining and allows quick flow out of the bottom of the pot.

JADE PLANT/MONEY PLANT
Crassula ovata

Size: Up to 1 foot tall   **Growth Habit:** Bushy   **Cost Rating:** $

NOT PET FRIENDLY

The Jade Plant is a common succulent-like plant that grows in a compact bush. Higher exposure to sun can bring reddish tips due to sun stress.

Care: The thick leaves and stems of the Jade Plant make this plant drought tolerant. Water the plant like you would a cactus or succulent—every 2 to 3 weeks or when the soil has been completely dried out for a few days. If you start to see the leaves crunch or shrivel, the plant is too dry. The Jade Plant enjoys high amounts of light and does well in a south- or west-facing window. The plant will stretch out without enough light. Clip back to prevent the stretching. Your soil mixture should be extremely well-draining and chunky to allow the roots to breathe and soil to dry out quickly. Cactus and succulent fertilizer are best suited to this plant.

Tip: Propagate cuttings easily by letting them callous over and planting them back in soil.

JANET CRAIG DRACAENA
Dracaena fragrans

Size: Up to 3 feet tall   **Growth Habit:** Upright   **Cost Rating:** $

NOT PET FRIENDLY

The Janet Craig Dracaena is a drought-tolerant plant characterized by clusters of pineapple-like leaves. The Dracaena genus is known for easy-to-care-for plants that are beginner-friendly. They are native to Africa and South America.

Care: The Janet Craig Dracaena can handle bright light but is better suited for indirect to low light in a north-facing window or pulled back from windows facing all other directions. Any plant should be watered in ratio to the amount of sun received, so if this plant is in a lower-light situation, watering won't be required as often. Let the soil dry out completely between waterings. Plant in a soil mixture similar to that of a cactus and succulent mix for optimal drainage.

MADAGASCAR DRAGON TREE

Dracaena marginata

Size: Up to 2+ feet tall   **Growth Habit:** Upright   **Cost Rating:** $

NOT PET FRIENDLY

The Madagascar Dragon Tree is a member of the beginner-friendly Dracaena genus. Best known for the barky stem and palm-like leaves that burst out of the top of the plant, the Madagascar Dragon Tree features long, slender leaves, sometimes with red details along the edges.

Care: This plant prefers to dry out significantly between waterings and has very few lighting requirements. If you have a darker space in your home, this plant is wonderful for that area. Your plant may develop brown leaf tips which is usually an indication the plant is putting out new growth. Use a well-draining, chunky soil mixture.

Tip: To help your Dragon Tree branch, deadhead and watch as new branches pop out. Growing new arms does take a while, so be patient!

MARBLE-QUEEN POTHOS

Epipremnum aureum

Size: Up to 2 feet long   **Growth Habit:** Climbing, Trailing   **Cost Rating:** $

NOT PET FRIENDLY

The Marble-Queen Pothos is one of the most common Pothos plant varieties, identified by the marbled variegation that covers the entire leaf. Under the right conditions, some leaves can turn out looking white. Let your Marble-Queen Pothos trail down, climb across the wall, or grow up a pole.

Care: For best results, give this plant plenty of bright indirect light in an east- or west-facing window, or pulled back from a south-facing exposure, even a little bit of direct morning sun as well, but watch for sunburn (see page 51). More light will encourage your plant to continue to put out highly variegated leaves. Plant in well-draining, chunky soil with additives like compost, orchid bark, pumice, and coco chips. Your Marble-Queen Pothos will indicate thirst by drooping her leaves downward. Use this cue to water thoroughly.

> **Tip:** Place small, clear command hooks along your wall. Guide the plant's stems into the hooks to encourage crawling across your walls.

MOONSHINE SNAKE PLANT

Dracaena trifasciata

Size: Up to 2 feet tall **Growth Habit:** Upright **Cost Rating:** $

NOT PET FRIENDLY

The Moonshine Snake Plant is best known for its pale green leaves. Dracaena are the classic tough-as-nails plant and can take really anything you throw at them, making them perfect for both the hands-on plant parent as well as the forgetful one.

Care: The Moonshine Snake Plant enjoys low to medium light, but if you want to see rapid growth, put this plant in higher-light situations. Use a well-draining soil mixture; something similar to a cactus and succulent mix would be perfect. The roots grow from rhizomes (modified stems running underground horizontally), which are excellent at holding water, making this plant highly drought tolerant. The leaves will begin to wrinkle when the plant is thirsty, but you should only have to water about every 3 to 4 weeks.

> **Did You Know:** Snake Plants have been used to make rope and even bandages because they are the perfect shape for dressing wounds.

OLD MAN CACTUS
Cephalocereus senilis

Size: Up to 2+ feet tall **Growth Habit:** Upright **Cost Rating:** $

NOT PET FRIENDLY

The Old Man Cactus has wild and unruly white "hair" that puffs up at the top of the plant and even down the sides. The "hair" helps the plant keep cool and protected from the sun in its native environment.

Care: The Old Man Cactus needs bright, direct light for multiple hours a day. A south-facing window is best. Water when the soil has been dry for a while, because the body of the cactus is a big reservoir. Plant your Old Man Cactus in a soil mixture that is extremely chunky and contains a minimal amount of compost. Water should run out the bottom of the pot immediately.

Tip: Plant your Old Man Cactus in a larger, shallow pot with other cacti to create a small cactus garden.

PAPER SPINE CACTUS

Tephrocactus articulatus var. papyracanthus

Size: Up to 1+ feet tall   **Growth Habit:** Upright   **Cost Rating:** $

NOT PET FRIENDLY

Cacti with the scientific name *Tephrocactus articulates* take on two different forms—one without spines, and one with. The Papyracanthus variant, or the Paper Spine Cactus, is known for long, soft spines that resemble a paper spine or long fingernails. The Pinecone Cactus is without spines and has a number of knobs.

Care: Both varieties of these plants enjoy high amounts of light from a south-facing window or direct sun outside. They do not need to be watered often, only about every 3 or 4 weeks, and not at all in the wintertime. Plant your cactus in a chunky, well-draining soil mixture. Make sure the water drains out of the pot immediately. Fertilize at the beginning and end of the growing season.

PARLOR PALM/NEANTHE BELLA PALM
Chamaedorea elegans

Size: Up to 3+ feet tall   **Growth Habit:** Upright   **Cost Rating:** $

NOT PET FRIENDLY

Native to Central America, the Parlor Palm became popularized during the Victorian era and continues to be one of the most common houseplants in the world. People would typically place this plant in their parlors for everyone to enjoy, hence their nickname.

Care: Most palms need a significant amount of light, but not this one. Place your Parlor Palm in the bright indirect light from a north-facing window or pulled back from an east- or west-facing window. The soil should be well-draining and slightly chunky to allow water to flow out of the bottom of the pot. The Parlor Palm doesn't like to dry out completely but also doesn't like the soil to remain saturated for too long. Keep the soil evenly moist, and water when the top 2 inches of soil are dried out. You won't need to fertilize your Parlor Palm more than a few times during the growing season.

Tip: Brown tips on palms are quite common, but you only should worry if the brown tips are growing larger; then the issue is likely due to watering.

PEACE LILY
Spathiphyllum (genus)

Size: Up to 2+ feet tall   **Growth Habit:** Upright   **Cost Rating:** $

NOT PET FRIENDLY

Peace Lilies are best known for their bold white flowers, but you'll want to keep them around for their deep green, shiny leaves. The Peace Lily is a particularly vocal plant when thirsty, drooping dramatically. These plants come in a solid green variety, but also in a variegated form called the Domino Peace Lily.

Care: Light requirements for the Peace Lily are quite simple: bright indirect light from an east-facing window, or pulled back from a west- or south-facing exposure. This plant is more likely to flower in higher light, but isn't particular otherwise. Hold off on watering your Peace Lily until you see drooping, a signal of being completely dried out. Your soil should be chunky and well-draining to allow the roots to breathe.

Did You Know: The Peace Lily flower is made up of a **spathe** and **spadix**, common flower anatomy for **aroids**.

PHILODENDRON BIRKIN

Philodendron hybrid

Size: Up to 1+ feet tall   **Growth Habit:** Upright   **Cost Rating:** $$

NOT PET FRIENDLY

The Philodendron Birkin is a recently popularized Philodendron **cultivar** with rounded, dark green leaves with lime green pinstripes. Sometimes the pinstripes can take over the majority of the leaf, giving it an almost white appearance. As a hybrid, the Birkin has generally unstable variegation and will revert to solid if not kept in optimal conditions.

Care: The Philodendron Birkin needs high amounts of bright indirect light—preferably near an east- or west-facing window—to maintain variegation. Like most other upright Philodendrons, the Birkin enjoys drying out a bit between waterings. Plant your Birkin in quick-draining soil; add in elements like pumice or orchid bark to help the mixture remain fluffy and chunky. Fertilize every few weeks during the growing season.

Did You Know: The Philodendron Birkin is not a naturally occurring plant, but rather a hybrid created through tissue culture.

PHILODENDRON BRASIL
Philodendron hybrid

Size: Up to 3+ feet long or tall   **Growth Habit:** Climbing, Trailing   **Cost Rating:** $

NOT PET FRIENDLY

The Philodendron Brasil is a cultivar of the *Philodendron hederaceum*. The leaves are dark green with bright green, yellow, or even white streaks running down the middle. With the variegation changing from leaf to leaf, you never know what the next leaf will look like.

Care: Philodendron Brasil will produce the most vibrant variegation with bright indirect light in an east- or west-facing window or pulled back from a south-facing exposure; however, the plant still thrives in lower light (such as in a north-facing window). Much like the other trailing Philodendrons, this plant can either cascade down or grow up a pole. Curling, much thinner, and more delicate leaves indicate thirst. To encourage bushy, full growth, prune the plant when stringy or smaller leaves begin appearing.

Did You Know: There are several forms of the Philodendron Brasil, including the Silver Stripe and the Rio Sport. All are characterized by their variegated, heart-shaped leaves.

PHILODENDRON PRINCE OF ORANGE
Philodendron hybrid

Size: Up to 1 foot tall   **Growth Habit:** Upright   **Cost Rating:** $

NOT PET FRIENDLY

The Philodendron Prince of Orange is an upright Philodendron hybrid. The leaves first come out a light orange color and eventually fade to deep green.

Care: The Prince of Orange is a simple plant to care for with minimal needs. Place your Prince of Orange in a bright area away from harsh sun rays, such as pulled back from east-, west-, or south-facing windows. Water when you notice the soil is almost or completely dried out. If the plant remains completely dried out for too many days, though, the lower leaves may yellow off. The Prince of Orange is generally a quick grower, so use your preferred fertilizer about every 2 weeks.

PICCOLO BANDA
Peperomia albovittata

Size: Up to 6 inches tall   **Growth Habit:** Upright   **Cost Rating:** $

PET FRIENDLY

The Piccolo Banda is a human-made Peperomia hybrid known for green leaves with dark red vertical stripes and bushy growth like most other Peperomia.

Care: Piccolo Banda does not need high amounts of light and will do better in indirect light, pulled back from an east- or west-facing window. A north-facing window is also a good option. Water this plant when the leaves become pliable and easy to bend. If overwatered, the stems will become mushy. Plant your Piccolo Banda in a well-draining soil mixture that helps retain moisture but does not stay soggy. Fertilize about once a month during the growing season.

POLKA-DOT PLANT/FRECKLE FACE
Hypoestes phyllostachya

Size: Up to 1 foot tall   **Growth Habit:** Bushy, Upright   **Cost Rating:** $

PET FRIENDLY

As the name suggests, the Polka-Dot Plant sports a polka-dotted pattern; colors of the plant vary from light to dark pink to white. As a member of the Acanthaceae family (along with Fittonia and Zebra Plant), the plant expresses its needs quite visibly and dramatically.

Care: Make sure the Polka-Dot Plant gets plenty of bright indirect light in an east- or west-facing window. If forced to stretch for light, this plant can easily become leggy and unattractive. Bright light in a south-facing window will also help maintain the bright colors. Plant your Polka-Dot Plant in soil that drains through right away but retains a bit more moisture. You only need to water your Polka-Dot Plant when you notice drooping. The plant might even trick you into thinking it's dead, but will "come back to life" after a big drink.

Tip: To keep your Polka-Dot Plant bushy and beautiful, prune when you notice longer spaces between leaves.

PONYTAIL PALM
Beaucarnea recurvata

Size: Up to 3+ feet tall   **Growth Habit:** Upright   **Cost Rating:** $$

PET FRIENDLY

The Ponytail Palm grows from a thick stem with long, curly leaves popping out of the top, much like a ponytail. Though they do well outside, Ponytail Palms can also be grown as houseplants. With the best conditions, over the course of many years, they can grow to be several feet tall with multiple branches.

Care: Ponytail Palms do well in high light, like a south- or west-facing window. This palm is best known for a thick, trunk-like stem, which helps the plant retain moisture. As such, you don't need to water the Ponytail Palm often, and, in fact, this plant enjoys drying out for quite a while. Plant your ponytail in a well-draining, chunky soil mixture similar to a succulent mixture.

Tip: Propagate the Ponytail Palm by cutting away offshoots from the stem, allowing them to callous over, and planting them in soil.

POTHOS NJOY

Epipremnum aureum

Size: Up to 3+ feet long   **Growth Habit:** Climbing, Trailing   **Cost Rating:** $

NOT PET FRIENDLY

The Pothos Njoy is a small-leafed variegated version of the *Epipremnum aureum*. The variegation shows up in green and white marbling. With leaves typically much smaller than those of other pothos, the Pothos Njoy is just as striking and makes a wonderful addition to any houseplant collection.

Care: The variegation means that the Pothos Njoy enjoys more light than other similar varieties. Plants with white margins or variegation are not able to photosynthesize as effectively as entirely green plants. Water your Pothos Njoy when the soil is completely dried out. Be sure not to allow "wet feet," or roots that stay wet for long periods of time. For this reason, plant in a well-draining, chunky soil mixture. Fertilize regularly to maintain consistent, healthy growth.

Did You Know: A similar plant is the Pearls and Jade, which is a cross between the Pothos Njoy and the Marble-Queen Pothos. The Pearls and Jade has speckles of variegation in the leaves' white margins, unlike the Pothos Njoy.

PURPLE HEART/PURPLE QUEEN
Tradescantia pallida

Size: Up to 3+ feet long   **Growth Habit:** Trailing   **Cost Rating:** $

NOT PET FRIENDLY

The Purple Heart is a trailing plant with large, deep purple leaves with a fuzzy layer. Generally, Tradescantia are known for having unique and colorful leaf patterns. In their native Mexico, they serve as ground cover. This trailing characteristic makes them wonderfully easy to propagate and grow in the home.

Care: The Purple Heart is a flexible plant able to handle a variety of lighting situations, from high to low. Provide the plant with a well-draining and chunky soil mixture and allow to completely dry out between waterings. Give a thorough soak when you do water, allowing water to flow out of the bottom of the pot.

> **Tip:** If your Purple Heart loses leaves toward the base of the plant, cut off stems from the length of the plant, root them in water, and plant them back into the pot for a fuller look.

REX BEGONIA
Begonia rex-cultorum

Size: Up to 1 foot tall   **Growth Habit:** Bushy   **Cost Rating:** $

NOT PET FRIENDLY

With flashy leaves and an easy nature, the Rex Begonia, native to Eastern Asia, is the most common household Begonia. These plants come in a variety of colors, sizes, and individual leaf shapes, which are typically asymmetrical.

Care: Place your Rex Begonia in indirect light, preferably near an east- or west-facing window or put outside under a shaded patio. This plant will wilt or droop when thirsty—hold off on watering until you see this indication. Fertilizing once or twice during the growing season should suffice. Rex Begonias can be propagated by leaf cutting; just place the leaf cutting in a nutrient-deficient mixture, keep it moist until roots begin to grow, then plant it.

Did You Know: The Escargot Begonia is a type of hybrid Rex Begonia with a spiral-shaped leaf, resembling a snail.

RIC-RAC CACTUS/FISHBONE CACTUS

Epiphyllum anguliger

Size: Up to 3+ feet long   **Growth Habit:** Hanging   **Cost Rating:** $

PET FRIENDLY

The Ric-Rac Cactus, otherwise known as the Fishbone Cactus, is a night-blooming cactus native to parts of Mexico. Known for a long, zig-zag leaf shape and easygoing nature, this plant has a similar growth habit to wild orchids, growing in clusters along the branches of trees.

Care: The Ric-Rac Cactus is a wonderful plant for beginners and is extremely forgiving. Make sure you plant it in a chunky, well-draining soil mixture and water it like you would a succulent, meaning thoroughly but only when the soil is completely dried out. For sunlight, this plant would be wonderfully happy on your covered patio, but an east- or west-facing window, or pulled back from a south-facing window, would suffice. Fertilize regularly to ensure consistent growth.

Did You Know: The Ric-Rac Cactus produces large pink and white flowers that only live for 24 hours. Though rarely seen, they are quite lovely if you ever get the chance.

SATIN POTHOS
Scindapsus pictus

Size: Up to 2+ feet tall   **Growth Habit:** Climbing, Trailing   **Cost Rating:** $$

NOT PET FRIENDLY

The Satin Pothos comes in many varieties with different levels of silver variegation. The common name Satin Pothos suggests that this plant is related to the Pothos (*Epipremnum*), but they are two entirely different species. This nickname is likely due to the similarity in growth habit between this plant and the Pothos.

Care: Though the Satin Pothos is tolerant of low light in a north-facing window, you'll see the most growth in an east-facing window. If you prefer to place the plant in south- or west-facing light, pull it back from the window. A well-draining, chunky soil mixture will serve this plant best. Wonderfully communicative, this plant's leaves curl inward when thirsty. Water deeply once you see the signs. Use organic fertilizer once a month during the growing season.

Did You Know: The botanical label "pictus" means painted, a reference to the leaf variegation resembling a painting.

SCARLET STAR
Guzmania lingulata

Size: Up to 1 foot tall **Growth Habit:** Upright **Cost Rating:** $

PET FRIENDLY

Scarlet Star is in the Bromeliad family, an extremely diverse group of plants with many shapes and sizes. This variety is best known for green foliage and a colorful flower head that resembles a star. Though commonly known as "Scarlet Star," the flower actually comes in many colors, including red, yellow, orange, and shades in between. The Scarlet Star is native to rainforests in Mexico, Central America, and the Caribbean.

Care: This plant needs bright light without direct sun rays falling onto the foliage. Best would be to place it pulled back from an east- or west-facing window. Bromeliads typically have a tank, which looks like a cup, in which they collect water. To water the plant, make sure the water levels in the "tank" are filled; also water the plant's soil sparingly. Scarlet Stars need to be watered with distilled or purified water. Bromeliads can grow in moss, bark, or soil. This plant does best with a foliar orchid fertilizer during growing season.

SILVER SWORD

Philodendron hastatum

Size: Up to 2+ feet tall   **Growth Habit:** Upright   **Cost Rating:** $$

NOT PET FRIENDLY

The Silver Sword, native to Brazil, has a greenish-gray hue. While the leaves can grow wide, they more commonly grow as thin, narrow leaves.

Care: The Silver Sword enjoys bright indirect light, pulled back from an east-, west-, or south-facing window. Water when the soil is about halfway dried out; the plant indicates thirst by drooping and hanging lower to the ground. Higher humidity is best, but not absolutely necessary. Use a well-draining soil mixture that is a bit better on moisture retention. Fertilize about once a month during the growing season.

SILVER TORCH

Cleistocactus strausii

Size: Up to 5+ feet tall   **Growth Habit:** Upright   **Cost Rating:** $$

PET FRIENDLY BUT IRRITATING

The Silver Torch is a captivating cactus species that grows in groups of long, silver columns and produces tall, cylindrical flowers. This cactus grows upright and very tall under the correct conditions.

Care: Much like other cacti, the Silver Torch needs bright direct light for a few hours a day. If indoors, place it in a south-facing window or, if outdoors, a partially covered patio or full sun will do. Water your cactus about once a month or when the soil has been dry for several days. In the winter, water less or not at all. This cactus needs an extremely well-draining and chunky soil mixture with minimal compost and lots of additives, like coco chips and pumice.

Tip: If this cactus doesn't receive enough light,
it will grow thinner when growing taller.

SNAKE PLANT/MOTHER-IN-LAW'S TONGUE
Dracaena trifasciata

Size: Up to 4+ feet tall **Growth Habit:** Upright **Cost Rating:** $

NOT PET FRIENDLY

The Snake Plant (formerly called scientifically *Sansevieria trifasciata*) is an incredibly durable and beginner-friendly houseplant known for long, sword-like leaves edged in bright yellow. This plant is equally as beautiful as it is simple and thrives off neglect.

Care: The Snake Plant is considered a low-light plant, but not a no-light plant. Though it's able to survive in low-light conditions that most plants could never, you'll see more consistent growth with higher light. This beginner-friendly and hardy plant is relaxed where watering is concerned. Thick tuberous roots serve as a water reservoir. You could go up to a month before this plant needs water again. Make sure your soil is well draining and closer to cactus soil in texture.

Did You Know: This plant has a few different common names, including "Mother-in-Law's Tongue."

SPIDER PLANT/AIRPLANE PLANT

Chlorophytum comosum

Size: Up to 1+ feet tall   **Growth Habit:** Bushy   **Cost Rating:** $

PET FRIENDLY

The Spider Plant, often seen in homes, offices, TV shows, and movies, comes in variegated leaves of green and white, solid green, and even curly green and white. The Spider Plant's common name comes from the plant's long, thin leaves and bushy growth that resembles spiders. Plantlets at the ends of long "webs" are easy to propagate.

Care: Spider Plants are happy in whatever lighting conditions suit you best—outside on a shaded patio or in a north-facing window in the living room. Drooping, leaves that fold up, or suddenly muted coloring are indications this plant is thirsty. The tuberous roots hold water for long periods of time, but the plant is thankful for deep watering when indicated. Well-draining soil is a must for this plant, essential to avoid root rot caused by water retention.

Did You Know: In addition to growing plantlets, this plant also produces small white flowers and seed pods.

STRING OF HEARTS/ROSARY VINE

Ceropegia woodii

Size: Up to 6+ feet long   **Growth Habit:** Trailing   **Cost Rating:** $$

PET FRIENDLY

As the name suggests, the String of Hearts has small, heart-shaped leaves along long stems. This quick-growing vine comes in green and variegated forms, the latter having the ability to make red, sun-stressed leaves when exposed to heavy light.

Care: The String of Hearts is best when treated like a succulent. The thick heart-shaped leaves store water for long amounts of time, so no need to water very often. When the soil is completely dried out and the plant needs water, the leaves will become thin and easily bendable. Water deeply, allowing the water to flow out of the bottom of the pot. Your String of Hearts needs lots of light, or the leaves will show less detail and grow in small. For lighting, try a covered patio or an east-, west-, or south-facing window. To ensure consistent growth, use an organic fertilizer at least once a month during the growing season.

Tip: You might find yourself giving your plant a haircut every couple of months to keep the growth under control. Share those pieces with your plant-loving friends!

SWISS CHEESE PLANT

Monstera deliciosa

Size: Up to 3+ feet tall   **Growth Habit:** Upright   **Cost Rating:** $$

NOT PET FRIENDLY

The Swiss Cheese Plant is one of the most iconic houseplants, and for good reason. As easy as they are beautiful, they make a welcome addition to any new houseplant collection. Young plants grow heart-shaped, solid leaves; they grow up to create awe-inspiring fenestrated leaves.

Care: Easily sunburned, this plant prefers medium light, such as in an east window or pulled back from a south- or west-facing window. Deeply water when the soil is almost completely dried out; you will see drooping, or leaves that become rippled along the edges when thirsty. Provide a well-draining, chunky soil mixture that allows room for the roots to breathe. Use an organic fertilizer once a month during the growing season to ensure prolific growth.

Tip: As an epiphyte, the Swiss Cheese Plant enjoys climbing trees in nature. Replicate this environment in your home by tethering the plant to a moss pole or strong trellis. Watch as the aerial roots dig into the pole and produce large mature leaves.

SYNGONIUM ARROWHEAD VINE
Syngonium podophyllum

Size: Up to 3+ feet tall   **Growth Habit:** Climbing, Trailing   **Cost Rating:** $

NOT PET FRIENDLY

Syngonium Arrowhead Vine is a climbing or trailing houseplant with arrow-shaped leaves. In its native habitat, this plant tends to be an invasive grower, which makes for fast-growing houseplants. With maturation, tri-leaf shapes begin to form. The Syngonium Arrowhead Vine features dark green leaves with lighter green highlights.

Care: The Syngonium Arrowhead Vine is highly adaptable to whatever sunlight you can provide, thriving just as well in a north-facing window as pulled back from a south-facing window, and everything in between. Let the well-draining soil mixture dry out completely between waterings, and watch for the plant's cue–drooping leaves–before watering. Train this plant to grow upright with a trellis. Pruning and propagating maintain bushy growth and allow the plant to trail down. Using an organic fertilizer monthly during the growing season will also help ensure prolific growth.

Did You Know: More than 30 different species of Syngonium have been found all the way from Mexico to Brazil.

SYNGONIUM PINK
Syngonium podophyllum

Size: Up to 1+ feet tall   **Growth Habit:** Upright   **Cost Rating:** $

NOT PET FRIENDLY

The Syngonium Pink is best known for pastel pink leaves with green undersides. As the plant matures, the leaves will get bigger and bigger and eventually begin to create a tri-leaf shape.

Care: The Syngonium Pink is tolerant to lower light, but keep it in bright indirect sunlight in an east- or west-facing window to maintain the vibrant pink color. Too much sunlight will bleach the leaves, so pulled back from direct light is best. Water when you see the leaves beginning to droop. Plant your Syngonium Pink in a soil mixture that allows for both moisture retention and proper drainage, using coco chips and perlite with any standard potting mix.

VARIEGATED OPUNTIA/VARIEGATED PRICKLY PEAR
Opuntia cochenillifera variegata

Size: Up to 1+ feet tall   **Growth Habit:** Upright   **Cost Rating:** $

NOT PET FRIENDLY

The Opuntia is a highly variant member of the cactus family, coming in many forms, shapes, sizes, and colors. The Variegated Opuntia is best known for varying and marbling colors anywhere from light to dark green, and even pink if exposed to high amounts of light.

Care: Your Variegated Opuntia will enjoy high amounts of light and would benefit from living outside or in a south-facing window inside. Make sure the soil is completely dried out in a timely manner between waterings. Use an extremely chunky and well-draining soil mixture made up mostly of pumice, coco chips, or other similar additives.

Tip: When your plant does not receive enough light, the pads will get long and skinny.

VELVET LEAF PHILODENDRON
Philodendron hederaceum

Size: Up to 2+ feet long or tall **Growth Habit:** Trailing **Cost Rating:** $

NOT PET FRIENDLY

The Velvet Leaf Philodendron (formerly *Philodendron micans*) is best known for its dark, velvety soft leaves. New growth comes in a wonderful light green and matures into a deep green, almost black, leaf. As with other trailing Philodendrons, you can train this plant upward or let it cascade down.

Care: Dark-leaf plants don't typically need as much light, so they do well in north-facing windows or pulled back from other windows. This plant visibly curls its leaves under when thirsty. Plant in well-draining soil. Water deeply until water drains out of the bottom of the pot. When allowed to trail, leaves may become progressively smaller. Prune the plant to keep a bushy growth. Use organic fertilizer regularly during the growing season.

> **Tip:** Plants in hanging baskets may not get as much light at the top of the plant and subsequently go bald. Wrap longer stems around the soil at the top of the pot and secure with bobby pins or paper clips to encourage them to take root and create more thickness.

WHITE GHOST EUPHORBIA/DRAGON BONE EUPHORBIA

Euphorbia lactea

Size: Up to 5+ feet tall   **Growth Habit:** Upright   **Cost Rating:** $$

NOT PET FRIENDLY

White Ghost Euphorbia is a form of Euphorbia native to Africa and often misidentified as cactus. This plant is best known for white and light green variegation.

Care: Though the White Ghost Euphorbia is not a cactus, the care is very similar. Plant it in a chunky, fast-draining soil and place in the highest light possible. This plant will do great under a covered patio or in direct sun after it's given a chance to acclimate. For indoor display, place your White Ghost Euphorbia in a south- or west-facing window. Water sparingly, only every couple of weeks. Propagate by cutting off a branch, letting it callous over for a few days, and planting it directly in soil.

Did You Know: The White Ghost Euphorbia will grow quite tall and branch with maturation.

XANADU
Thaumatophyllum xanadu

Size: Up to 3+ feet tall   **Growth Habit:** Upright   **Cost Rating:** $

NOT PET FRIENDLY

The Xanadu is a miniature version of the *Thaumatophyllum selloum*. This plant features a round, hand-like leaf shape that follows the sun and has big, chunky stems with oval markings where old leaves grew previously.

Care: The Xanadu is happy to live in the bright light of a south- or east-facing window. Water when the soil is dry about halfway down; make sure to evenly saturate the soil so all parts of the root ball receive moisture. Use a well-balanced, quick-draining soil mixture that allows for moisture retention and drainage. Fertilize the Xanadu about once a month during the growing season.

Tip: The leaves will stretch to face one direction to receive as much light as possible. Rotate your plant every week or so to avoid asymmetrical growth.

ZEBRA PLANT
Aphelandra squarrosa

Size: Up to 1 foot tall **Growth Habit:** Upright **Cost Rating:** $

PET FRIENDLY

The Zebra Plant is a member of the particularly communicative Acanthaceae plant family known for their striking, patterned foliage and ability to "die" and come back to life. When thirsty, these plants will droop heavily, almost to the point of looking dead. The Zebra Plant's name comes from the bold white stripes against deep green leaves.

Care: The Zebra plant isn't picky about location and doesn't require high light. Place your Zebra plant pulled back from an east-, west-, or south-facing window, or on the windowsill of a north-facing window. Plant in a well-draining soil mixture that helps retain moisture. When thirsty, this typically rigid plant will become soft and droopy. Water thoroughly and watch as the plant "comes back to life."

Did You Know: Other members of this plant family include the Nerve Plant and the Polka-Dot Plant.

ZZ
Zamioculcas zamiifolia

Size: Up to 3+ feet tall **Growth Habit:** Upright **Cost Rating:** $

NOT PET FRIENDLY

The *Zamioculcas zamiifolia*, more commonly known as ZZ, is a wonderful multi-stem plant. New leaf stalks emerge from the soil as one, and slowly open, revealing thick, dark green leaves.

Care: The laid-back ZZ plant prefers medium light but is happy in low-light conditions. This plant grows out of large tubers, which hold water for long periods of time. Water once every few weeks to a month, depending on the size of the plant. Soil should be well-draining, allowing water to quickly run out of the bottom of the pot.

Tip: Propagate the ZZ plant by stem-cutting or leaf-cutting and placing the cuttings in water until you see roots and a tuber forming.

Chapter 7

MEDIUM-MAINTENANCE PLANTS

AIR PLANT

Tillandsia xerographica

Size: Up to 8 inches tall   **Growth Habit:** Epiphyte   **Cost Rating:** $

PET FRIENDLY

The *Tillandsia xerographica*, native to Mexico and South America, is large and dome-shaped. This plant does not need to grow in soil because the air provides all the nutrients the plant needs. The Air Plant is relatively slow-growing and mostly germinates from seed.

Care: The Air Plant is happy to live in bright sun and can even handle bits of direct light. Saturate this plant about once a week in distilled water for 1 to 3 hours and let it sit upside down to dry. Distilled water is necessary because the plant is sensitive to chlorine and minerals in tap water. Use a foliar fertilizer about once a month after you water.

> **Tip:** This plant does not tolerate staying wet for too long. After watering, set it upside down so all the water can drain out.

ALBO ARROWHEAD VINE

Syngonium podophyllum albo-variegata

Size: Up to 2+ feet tall   **Growth Habit:** Upright   **Cost Rating:** $$

NOT PET FRIENDLY

The Albo Arrowhead Vine is a white-variegated Syngonium with unpredictable marble variegation. Each leaf will be completely unique—you never know what you'll get.

Care: The Albo Arrowhead Vine does well in cool, bright exposure from an east window. The white variegation is best maintained with high light. New growth comes in light and dark green, but eventually the light green parts will fade into a wonderful creamy white color. Water when you notice leaves beginning to droop. Plant in a well-draining and chunky soil mixture that allows for drainage as well as moisture retention. Fertilize regularly for prolific growth.

ALOCASIA FRYDEK/ALOCASIA GREEN VELVET
Alocasia micholitziana

Size: Up to 2+ feet tall   **Growth Habit:** Upright   **Cost Rating:** $$

NOT PET FRIENDLY

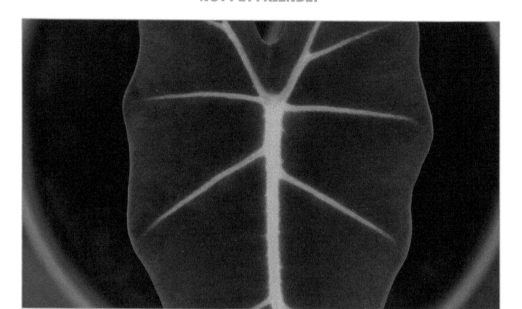

The Alocasia Frydek is a stunning member of the Alocasia genus. This plant is best known for its dark green arrowhead-shaped leaves with light green veins.

Care: The Alocasia Frydek is an understory plant in the wild, so it does not need high amounts of light. The dark leaves also help more readily with photosynthesis. This plant needs and loves humidity. Plant in a soil good for both moisture retention and drainage. A mixture of compost, orchid bark, and perlite would suffice. Water your Frydek when the top 1 to 2 inches of soil are dry, because this plant does not like to dry out.

Tip: If the Alocasia Frydek does not receive enough humidity, the leaves will develop brown tips.

ALOCASIA POLLY/AFRICAN MASK
Alocasia amazonica

Size: Up to 1 foot tall **Growth Habit:** Upright **Cost Rating:** $

NOT PET FRIENDLY

The Alocasia Polly is striking with large, shiny foliage, dark in color with light veins and a crinkled texture. The backs of the leaves are a dark purple. This plant is one of the more finicky varieties of Alocasia.

Care: The Alocasia Polly benefits from indirect light, such as when pulled back from windows, and is highly susceptible to sunburn. In the wild, this plant grows in damp, humid environments. Replicate the natural habitat as best you can by providing a moisture-retaining soil mixture that allows drainage, such as with coco-peat-based mixes that include compost and perlite. Don't let the soil dry out more than 1 to 2 inches down. Alocasia, in general, enjoy high amounts of humidity, above 50 percent. This plant may go completely dormant and lose all its leaves. The leaves will regrow; keep watering the bulb as usual. Fertilize once a month.

Did You Know: Alocasia plants grow from bulbs. Stored energy in the bulb deep in the soil is used in the next growing season.

ASPARAGUS FERN

Asparagus retrofractus

Size: Up to 6 inches tall **Growth Habit:** Bushy, Trailing **Cost Rating:** $

NOT PET FRIENDLY

The Asparagus Fern features long, thin stems accompanied by small, soft, and straight leaves. This plant is quite commonly found both inside and outside.

Care: The Asparagus Fern needs bright indirect light in an east-facing window or pulled back from a west- or south-facing window. If outside, place on shaded patios. The feather-like leaves are prone to shedding when not receiving the light and water they need. Water when the soil is dried out. The plant's tuberous roots will hold on to water but won't tolerate drying out for too long. Provide high amounts of humidity to maintain foliage—above 45 percent is preferred.

Did You Know: Despite the name, this plant is not a fern but a part of the Liliaceae family.

BIRDS NEST FERN
Asplenium nidus

Size: Up to 6 inches tall   **Growth Habit:** Upright   **Cost Rating:** $

PET FRIENDLY

Unsurprisingly, the Birds Nest Fern resembles a bird's nest. Each new long and skinny frond grows out from the center of the plant. The edges of the leaves are rippled and light green. In nature, this plant can grow on the ground or in trees.

Care: The Birds Nest Fern prefers indirect light, pulled back from windows and away from harsh sun rays. Choose a well-draining soil that retains some moisture. Water when the soil is dry 1 to 2 inches down; ferns don't enjoy drying out completely and benefit from having some moisture (though not saturation) in the soil.

Did You Know: Ferns do not produce flowers and seeds; rather, they reproduce via spores generated through the leaves.

BLACK GOLD PHILODENDRON
Philodendron melanochrysum

Size: Up to 2+ feet tall **Growth Habit:** Upright **Cost Rating:** $$$

NOT PET FRIENDLY

The Black Gold Philodendron is becoming increasingly popular. Best known for long, velvety leaves that get bigger and bigger with each new leaf. The dark foliage and light green veining make this plant a total showstopper.

Care: Because the leaves are darker, this plant doesn't need as much light as others. Though happy to live pulled back from most windows, the Black Gold Philodendron benefits from bright indirect light in an east- or west-facing window. The Black Gold Philodendron thrives in high-humidity environments above 50 percent, but it will fare better the more you can provide. Plant in a chunky soil mixture that allows the roots to breathe, and provide a moss pole for the plant to climb. Water the plant when the leaves feel softer and thinner to the touch, or when the top 2 or 3 inches of the soil are dry.

Did You Know: The mature Black Gold Philodendron can produce leaves up to 2 feet long.

CALADIUM/ANGEL WINGS

Caladium bicolor

Size: Up to 1 foot tall   **Growth Habit:** Upright   **Cost Rating:** $

NOT PET FRIENDLY

Caladiums are a perennial houseplant grown from bulbs and known for their colorful and striking foliage. Usually sold in stores at the beginning of spring, Caladium plants produce leaves from spring to fall but go dormant in the wintertime, losing all their leaves.

Care: When caring for a Caladium indoors, avoid exposing the plant to harsh sun rays; best is a north- or east-facing window. Water your Caladium when the soil is about halfway dried out. Avoid drought periods while the plant is actively growing. Your soil should be well-draining. Use your preferred fertilizer about every 2 weeks during the growing season.

CALATHEA FREDDIE

Goeppertia concinna

Size: Up to 1 foot tall   **Growth Habit:** Bushy   **Cost Rating:** $

PET FRIENDLY

Goeppertia are more difficult plants until you have created the right environment. The extra effort is worth the trouble because these plants are beautiful to have around. The Calathea Freddie (formerly *Calathea concinna*) features long, pointed light green leaves with symmetrically patterned, dark green stripes. The leaves canopy over one another for a full, bushy plant.

Care: The Calathea Freddie prefers a shaded spot. Pull back from bright windows and direct sun because the sensitive foliage is prone to sunburn. To prevent brown tips or curly edges, plant in soil that retains moisture, but drains well. Water when the soil is dry 1 to 2 inches down, depending on pot size. This plant prefers distilled or filtered water, since tap water may burn the leaf edges and turn them brown. Like other Calathea plants, the Freddie enjoys high humidity above 50 percent.

> **Tip:** You may be tempted to mist the leaves to provide more humidity, but this short-term solution may invite in bacteria and dust. Instead, consider placing your Calathea Freddie on a humidity tray, near a humidifier, or in a humid room like the bathroom.

CALATHEA ORBIFOLIA
Goeppertia orbifolia

Size: Up to 8+ inches tall   **Growth Habit:** Bushy   **Cost Rating:** $$

PET FRIENDLY

Plants in the Goeppertia genus are known as "diva-esque" plants that will let you know when they are unhappy. The Calathea Orbifolia tends to be a more laid-back genus member, slightly more forgiving. Known for round, faintly striped leaves that grow outward like a bouquet, these plants are a great introduction to Goeppertia and will reward you richly under the right conditions.

Care: The Calathea Orbifolia demands a specific environment with humidity levels above 50 percent at all times. Watering with distilled or reverse osmosis water will help prevent brown tips due to leaf burn. Choose a well-draining soil that allows some moisture. Don't let the soil dry out more than halfway to ensure proper growth and full green leaves.

Tip: To help increase the moisture around your plant, create a large humidity tray (page 28).

CHINESE MONEY PLANT/PANCAKE PLANT
Pilea peperomioides

Size: Up to 8+ inches tall   **Growth Habit:** Upright   **Cost Rating:** $$

PET FRIENDLY

The Chinese Money Plant has prolific growth habits. Pick up a pot of this plant and you'll likely find one or two babies growing in the soil. The succulent UFO-looking disk leaves make for wonderful visual interest.

Care: You'll serve this plant best by treating it much like you would a succulent—watering deeply only after the soil has completely dried, and providing plenty of light from an east-, west-, or south-facing window. Plant in a well-draining, chunky soil mixture, and to ensure prolific growth, use an organic fertilizer monthly during the growing season.

> **Tip:** When you see new babies emerging from the soil or growing along the main stem, allow them to form 4 or 5 leaves before separating them from the mother plant. Do so by gently digging them up or cutting them at the surface of the soil or stem, and root them in water.

DUMB CANE
Dieffenbachia seguine

Size: Up to 2+ feet   **Growth Habit:** Upright   **Cost Rating:** $

NOT PET FRIENDLY

The Dieffenbachia, or Dumb Cane, is a popular houseplant with striking foliage. There are several forms of the Dumb Cane, all boasting variegated patterned leaves. The Dumb Cane grows in thick stalks, resembling sugar cane. The name "Dumb Cane" comes from the temporary speechlessness that results from eating the toxic stem, which causes inflammation and numbness of the tongue and throat.

Care: This highly adaptable houseplant can live in myriad conditions. Whether you have high-light or low-light availability, this plant should be happy. Let the soil dry out halfway between waterings, and make sure the soil mixture is well-draining and chunky.

Tip: If the plant develops a long, empty stem, cut off the stem to propagate and start over.

FIDDLE-LEAF FIG
Ficus lyrata

Size: Up to 6+ feet tall **Growth Habit:** Upright **Cost Rating:** $$

NOT PET FRIENDLY

The Fiddle-Leaf Fig, one of the most popular members of the Ficus genus, is best known for leaves that resemble a small violin, hence the name. This tree, especially as a larger plant, is wonderful for creating visual interest and a bold statement.

Care: The Fiddle-Leaf Fig prefers high light and consistently warm temperatures inside your home or under the shade of your patio and prefers south-, east-, or west-facing windows. Soil must be well-draining. Thoroughly water the plant from the top when the soil is halfway dried out, and maintain a regular schedule because the plant enjoys a consistent watering routine. Use an organic fertilizer once a month during the growing season to ensure prolific growth. Though not needing high humidity, this plant does best when provided with 40 percent humidity or more.

Tip: Don't be afraid to prune! Doing so will encourage new branches for a fuller plant more closely resembling a tree.

FLAMINGO LILY/PAINTER'S PALETTE
Anthurium andraeanum

Size: Up to 1 foot tall **Growth Habit:** Upright **Cost Rating:** $

NOT PET FRIENDLY

The Flamingo Lily, native to tropical areas of Central and South America, is the most common form of Anthurium. This plant is best known for the bright colored, waxy flowers that are typically red, pink, or white, with a yellow spadix. The foliage is heart-shaped and deep green.

Care: The Flamingo Lily is susceptible to sunburn and so enjoys filtered and bright indirect light in east- or west-facing windows, or being pulled back from a south-facing exposure. Plant your Flamingo Lily in a soil mixture that allows for drainage as well as moisture retention. Add in perlite or orchid bark to improve the quality. Water your plant when the top inch or so of the soil is dry, keeping the plant evenly moist but not soaking wet.

Did You Know: The Flamingo Lily flowers are made up of a combination of spathes and spadix.

GOLD DUST CROTON
Codiaeum variegatum

Size: Up to 1+ feet tall   **Growth Habit:** Upright   **Cost Rating:** $

NOT PET FRIENDLY

The Gold Dust Croton is a member of the greater Codiaeum genus, a collection of plants known for brightly colored foliage. You might have seen a member of the Codiaeum genus in the shopping mall, offices, or other similar places. The Gold Dust Croton has long, thin green leaves sprinkled with gold flecks.

Care: For best results, provide with high light from a south-facing window. This plant needs multiple hours of direct light to thrive and maintain the gold-dust look. The Gold Dust Croton will droop when thirsty. The high amounts of sunlight mean the plant's water will likely dry up very quickly. Plant in a well-draining, chunky soil mixture that allows the water to run out of the pot immediately.

Tip: To propagate the Gold Dust Croton, cut off a stem, remove the lower leaves, and place the stem in water until roots begin to form.

GOLDEN MOSAIC
Ctenanthe lubbersiana

Size: Up to 1+ feet tall   **Growth Habit:** Upright   **Cost Rating:** $$

PET FRIENDLY

The Golden Mosaic is a member of the larger Marantaceae family with similar traits to other prayer plants, like curling up when thirsty and folding up in the evenings. The leaves are long and ovate with yellow-gold patches or stripes and emerge from long, skinny stems that grow straight up.

Care: The Golden Mosaic is considered a lower-light plant. Use a soil mixture that retains moisture yet drains well. Always water your plants in ratio to how much light they get, as when placed in a lower-light spot, the Golden Mosaic will use less water. Only water when the top inch or so of the soil is dried out.

Tip: The Golden Mosaic propagates easily by cutting underneath a node and submerging in soil or other propagation **substrate**. Once roots have formed, plant in soil.

HEART LEAF FERN
Hemionitis arifolia

Size: Up to 4 inches tall   **Growth Habit:** Bushy   **Cost Rating:** $

PET FRIENDLY

The Heart Leaf Fern is a dwarf from Southeast Asia. Small, heart-shaped leaves grow from fuzzy stems. With a growth habit low to the ground, this plant is suitable for living within or outside a terrarium.

Care: The Heart Leaf Fern needs indirect light in a north-facing window or a spot pulled away from windows facing other directions to avoid harsh sun rays. The best soil mixture is well-draining but able to retain moisture, so a bit heavier in coco peat. Soil should be kept moist, but not soggy. As a fern, this plant needs high amounts of humidity. Above 50 percent is ideal for minimizing brown and crispy leaves.

Tip: Heart Leaf Ferns are typically sold as small plants, making them ideal for placement under a small cloche (glass covering) or inside a terrarium.

HOYA HINDU ROPE
Hoya carnosa compacta

Size: Up to 1+ feet long   **Growth Habit:** Trailing   **Cost Rating:** $–$$

NOT PET FRIENDLY WITH EXCEPTIONS

The sought-after *Hoya carnosa compacta*, nicknamed Hoya Hindu Rope, is a mutation of the common *Hoya carnosa* but with a special beauty. Available in both variegated and dark green forms, this plant is known for compacted, curly leaves that resemble tortellini pasta on a rope. New growth emerges as tiny, fuzzy pink leaves and develops into beautiful green clusters.

Care: Hoyas require high light from an east-, west-, or south-facing window. This plant will produce more growth in higher ambient humidity (40 percent and up). Plant your Hoya Hindu Rope in a well-draining, bark-heavy soil mixture so the roots have plenty of space to breathe. This plant's leaves are thick and succulent and, when thirsty, will wrinkle.

Did You Know: This plant produces large spherical blooms comprising many different individual flowers. Some say they smell like chocolate and are most fragrant at night.

HOYA LINEARIS

Hoya linearis

Size: Up to 3+ feet long   **Growth Habit:** Trailing   **Cost Rating:** $–$$

NOT PET FRIENDLY WITH EXCEPTIONS

The unique Hoya Linearis could almost be mistaken for a jungle cactus, but the white umbel-shaped (branching out from a single point) flowers leave no doubt of this plant's Hoya genus identity. The leaves are fuzzy and soft, though be careful petting them because they are quite delicate.

Care: This plant requires much different care than other popular Hoyas, especially with lighting and water. The Hoya Linearis is happy to live in dappled light pulled back from an east-, west-, or south-facing window. Don't let the soil dry out completely; rather, water when about halfway dry. Well-draining soil is still a must, so the roots can breathe and not hold too much water for too long.

> **Tip:** To propagate, cut between the stems above each individual leaf node, and place into moist soil or moss. A highly humid environment like a closed container or greenhouse will also help ensure success.

JEWEL ORCHID
Ludisia discolor

Size: Up to 6+ inches tall   **Growth Habit:** Upright   **Cost Rating:** $$

PET FRIENDLY

The *Ludisia discolor* is a type of Jewel Orchid with dark, almost black, foliage and pink stripes. The bottoms of the leaves are dark red, and they will sometimes put out white flowers from spikes. This type of orchid, called a **terrestrial** orchid, can grow in soil. The Jewel Orchid grows as an understory plant in parts of Asia.

Care: The Jewel Orchid is best known for dark foliage, indicating the plant doesn't need high amounts of light. The Jewel Orchid is happy pulled back from windows where the foliage can avoid any direct light. For watering, make sure the soil never completely dries. Water your plant when the top inch or so of the soil is dry, and use well-draining soil to prevent the roots from staying saturated for too long. Use a basic orchid fertilizer for best results.

KING ANTHURIUM

Anthurium veitchii

Size: Up to 1+ feet tall   **Growth Habit:** Climbing, Epiphyte   **Cost Rating:** $$$$

NOT PET FRIENDLY

The King Anthurium is among the most striking of the Anthurium plants for its long leaf shape and rippled texture. In Colombia, where the King Anthurium grows wild, the leaves can reach up to 6 feet long.

Care: The King Anthurium should be treated similarly to the Swiss Cheese Plant (page 114). As an epiphyte, this plant is accustomed to receiving more light than other members of the Anthurium genus and will do well pulled back in east-, west-, or south-facing windows. Use a very well-draining, airy soil so the roots can breathe. When watered, the leaves are stiff and sturdy; thirsty leaves will have a duller color and feel thinner to the touch, which is your cue to water deeply, ensuring that water drains out the bottom of the pot. This plant benefits from ambient humidity above 40 percent.

Tip: Try growing this plant in a hanging orchid basket,
and watch as the beautiful leaves splay.

MINI MONSTERA
Rhaphidophora tetrasperma

Size: Up to 5+ feet tall   **Growth Habit:** Upright   **Cost Rating:** $$$

NOT PET FRIENDLY

The Mini Monstera is gaining popularity in the houseplant community and can be hard to find. This plant is smaller than the *Monstera deliciosa* (Swiss Cheese Plant), its namesake due to their resemblance. The Mini Monstera is a fast grower and does best in an upright position. With time and maturity, this plant will produce secondary "mid-rib" **fenestrations**.

Care: The Mini Monstera prefers higher light in an east-, west-, or south-facing window. A quick-growing climbing plant, it needs support from a trellis or bamboo stake. This plant will droop when thirsty; water thoroughly once the soil is almost completely dried out. The Mini Monstera needs a well-draining, chunky soil mixture. Don't be afraid to prune or propagate and share with others! When the plant is pruned, a new branch will shoot out within a few weeks. Use an organic fertilizer monthly during the growing season for prolific growth.

Did You Know: The Mini Monstera has become widely available due to tissue culture, the process of cloning a plant from tissues or cells, allowing for a large number of one plant to be produced faster than through other forms of propagation.

MISTLETOE CACTUS
Rhipsalis baccifera

Size: Up to 1+ feet long   **Growth Habit:** Trailing, Epiphyte   **Cost Rating:** $$$

NOT PET FRIENDLY

The Mistletoe Cactus is a jungle cactus native to South and Central America and parts of Africa.

Care: As an epiphyte, the Mistletoe Cactus needs a chunkier soil mixture with components like orchid bark, pumice, and compost. Not necessarily needing bright direct light, this plant does benefit from brighter light throughout the day but can also grow happily in more medium light, in or pulled back from east-, west-, or south-facing windows. How often you water will depend on how much light the plant gets; every few weeks is usually suitable. The stems retain moisture, indicating a bit more drought tolerance.

Did You Know: This plant's small flowers later produce berries. To propagate by seed, plant the berries, or to simply propagate, cut off a few pieces and plant them directly into soil.

MONSTERA PERU/MONSTERA KARSTENIANUM

Monstera sp. Peru

Size: Up to 2+ feet tall   **Growth Habit:** Climbing, Trailing   **Cost Rating:** $$

NOT PET FRIENDLY

The Monstera Peru has bold foliage best-known for deep green, puckered leaves. This plant can trail but is best shown off as a climbing plant. The more mature the plant gets, the bigger and better the leaves will become.

Care: The Monstera Peru is a trickier member of the Monstera genus but certainly not out of bounds for a beginner. The Monstera Peru likes high to medium light, pulled back from an east-, west-, or south-facing window. The best growth is fostered by letting the Monstera Peru climb up a pole. Plant in a well-draining, chunky mix suitable for epiphytes. With the right conditions, this plant can be a quick grower and satisfying to watch mature.

Tip: The thick, waxy leaves indicate this plant holds
on to water for longer than thin-leaf plants.

MONSTERA SILTEPECANA/SILVER MONSTERA
Monstera siltepecana

Size: Up to 2 feet long **Growth Habit:** Climbing, Trailing **Cost Rating:** $$

NOT PET FRIENDLY

The Monstera Siltepecana is a small-leaf trailing Monstera plant with elongated, heart-shaped leaves that have light green to silver markings. The leaves are textured and can appear puckered and bumpy.

Care: This plant does best with an eastern exposure where small amounts of direct light can reach the foliage before the outside gets too hot. Cool, bright light will encourage the plant to continue putting out variegated leaves. Water when the soil is about halfway dried out. This plant doesn't enjoy drying out completely and will indicate excessive thirst by drooping. Plant in a well-draining soil mixture ideal for tropical houseplants, with components such as coco chips, pumice, and coco peat that allow pockets of moisture within mostly dry soil. Fertilize regularly, as this plant grows quickly.

MOONLIGHT
Scindapsus treubii

Size: Up to 2 feet tall   **Growth Habit:** Climbing, Trailing   **Cost Rating:** $$$

NOT PET FRIENDLY

The Moonlight is a trailing member of the Scindapsus genus. Best known for light green, rubbery leaves, this unique plant makes a wonderful addition to any indoor garden.

Care: The *Scindapsus treubii* "Moonlight" enjoys bright indirect light in an east- or west-facing window and can even handle small bits of direct light in the morning. In nature, this plant enjoys climbing up trees and along the rainforest floor, so you may want to try providing a moss pole. Plant in a well-draining and chunky soil mixture. Add in orchid bark, coco chips, and pumice for a well-rounded soil mixture. Water when the leaves begin to curl under, the plant's indication of thirst. Fertilize regularly, about once a month.

MOTH ORCHID
Phalaenopsis amabilis

Size: Up to 2 feet tall   **Growth Habit:** Upright   **Cost Rating:** $

PET FRIENDLY

The Moth Orchid is a common orchid frequently given as gifts. This plant comes in a larger or mini form and in a multitude of colors. Rather than being planted in soil, these orchids are unique in that they prefer bark. Moth Orchids are epiphytes and, in nature, grow on the branches of tall trees.

Care: To water, soak your Moth Orchid's roots in a cup of water for 15 to 20 minutes and avoid getting the leaves wet to avoid rotting. The plant indicates thirst by changing color from green to more of a gray. Monitor the roots to avoid letting them get dry. Over time, you'll learn the interval at which your orchid needs water—typically, around once a week. Plant in orchid bark with a small amount of moss for optimal air flow—orchids will not do well in traditional soil unless the plant is a terrestrial orchid variety. Use a foliar orchid fertilizer after the plant has finished blooming—don't spray the flowers.

Tip: Once your orchid has bloomed, keep up the same care. A new flower will come though this process but could take up to 6 months.

NERVE PLANT/MOSAIC PLANT

Fittonia albivenis

Size: Up to 8 inches tall **Growth Habit:** Bushy **Cost Rating:** $

PET FRIENDLY

The Nerve Plant is a popular houseplant with small, veiny foliage. This plant is quite dramatic when thirsty, drooping so much that it appears dead. After a quick drink, however, this plant looks as good as new.

Care: The Nerve Plant does well in a north-facing window, or pulled back from an east-, west-, or south-facing exposure. A well-draining soil mixture is essential for your plant to grow strong. With a bushy growth habit, this plant needs regular pruning to avoid legginess. Simply pop what you prune off into water and watch new roots form. Once the plant droops with thirst, water right away or you'll risk losing leaves. A thorough and deep watering should perk the plant right back up.

Did You Know: The Nerve Plant comes in many different colors and leaf sizes, from small, dark green foliage with white veins, to large, dark burgundy foliage with pink veins.

NORFOLK ISLAND PINE/STAR PINE
Araucaria heterophylla

Size: Up to 4+ feet tall   **Growth Habit:** Upright   **Cost Rating:** $$
NOT PET FRIENDLY

The Norfolk Island Pine is a popular holiday plant and makes a particularly lovely living Christmas tree. Their unique structure is a wonderful statement piece in any home.

Care: The Norfolk Island Pine enjoys bright indirect sunlight to prevent sunburn. Place in an east- or west-facing window or pulled back from a south-facing exposure. These plants are not cold-tolerant, so if you live where the temperatures drop below 55 degrees Fahrenheit, be sure to keep them inside. Choose a well-draining soil that retains some moisture. The Norfolk Island Pine benefits from ambient humidity of 40 percent or higher and does not like to dry out. Water once the soil is about halfway dry.

Did You Know: The Norfolk Island Pine is native to Norfolk Island in the South Pacific Ocean. Despite the name, this plant is not actually a pine, but a conifer.

PEPEROMIA SILVER FROST

Peperomia griseoargentea

Size: Up to 1 foot tall **Growth Habit:** Upright **Cost Rating:** $

PET FRIENDLY

Though Peperomia can be sensitive, the Peperomia Silver Frost is typically easy to care for, clear about needs, and easy to propagate. The Silver Frost is best known for a silver, sparkly sheen.

Care: The Silver Frost doesn't need a ton of light; in fact, these plants are happy to be pulled back from bright east- or west-facing windows because their foliage is usually quite sensitive. Though the Silver Frost is a bit hardier, the plant is still a Peperomia. The leaves will become soft and pliable when the plant needs a drink—wait for this cue to water. Plant your Silver Frost in a well-draining mixture that retains a bit more moisture, but still drains quickly and allows the roots to breathe properly. Fertilize regularly.

PHILODENDRON BRANDI/SILVER LEAF PHILODENDRON
Philodendron brandtianum

Size: Up to 2+ feet long **Growth Habit:** Climbing, Trailing **Cost Rating:** $$

NOT PET FRIENDLY

Heart-shaped leaves with a smattering of silver flecks are what make the Philodendron Brandi unique.

Care: The Philodendron Brandi will grow happiest in bright indirect sunlight such as in an east- or west-facing window or pulled back from a south-facing exposure. Bright light will keep the plant producing silvery flecks. This plant does not enjoy completely drying out, so water thoroughly when you find the first few inches of soil are dry. This plant will also indicate thirst by drooping or curling leaves. Plant in a well-draining and chunky soil. Fertilize every few weeks during the growing season.

Tip: Let this plant trail down or grow up a moss pole.

PHILODENDRON GLORIOSUM
Philodendron hybrid

Size: Up to 2 feet tall   **Growth Habit:** Creeping   **Cost Rating:** $$

NOT PET FRIENDLY

The Philodendron Gloriosum is a large-leaf Philodendron variety with a creeping growth habit. In nature, these plants can be found crawling across the ground, rather than climbing up trees or other surroundings. Their soft velvet leaves become larger and larger with growth.

Care: The Philodendron Gloriosum is deceivingly easy to care for. The plant does best in indirect light of east- and west-facing windows, pulled back from harsh sun rays. Plant it in a chunky, well-draining soil mixture. As a creeping plant, the Philodendron Gloriosum has a tendency to grow low to the pot rather than upward. To keep growth under control, propagate by cutting between nodes. After you make a cut, the plant will start to grow another branch. Fertilize regularly to ensure consistent growth.

Did You Know: Philodendron are known for their leaf variability—known as variation and morphogenesis—from plant to plant. With this variability, though two specimens of the same species look different, they are the same species nonetheless.

PHILODENDRON MAMEI

Philodendron hybrid

Size: Up to 1+ feet tall   **Growth Habit:** Creeping   **Cost Rating:** $$$$

NOT PET FRIENDLY

The Philodendron Mamei is a big-leaf, heart-shaped philodendron known for a rich green color with silver splashes. This variety, though sometimes difficult to find, is wonderfully rewarding with growth. You will be dazzled as you watch new leaves form and emerge, each unique and larger than the last.

Care: As a creeping plant, the Philodendron Mamei does not receive high light in the natural habitat. Consequently, this plant will do well pulled back from an east-, west-, or south-facing window. To maintain beautiful foliage, the Mamei should live in high ambient humidity (50 percent or more). As with many philodendrons, this plant will rip its own leaf in an attempt to unfurl without enough humidity. The Philodendron Mamei needs well-draining, chunky soil and should be watered when the soil is at least halfway dried out. The leaves will droop with thirst.

Did You Know: The structure from which a new Mamei leaf emerges is called a cataphyll. The purpose of this structure is to protect the newly developing and growing leaf.

PHILODENDRON PINK PRINCESS
Philodendron erubescens

Size: Up to 3+ feet tall   **Growth Habit:** Upright   **Cost Rating:** $$$

NOT PET FRIENDLY

The Philodendron Pink Princess is a highly popular and sought-after houseplant with large leaves that have pink splashes. Even the sap is pink! New leaves emerge bright pink with splatches of almost black and mature to a lighter pink and deeper green color.

Care: The Philodendron Pink Princess enjoys living in bright indirect light in an east- or west-facing window or pulled back from a south-facing exposure. To keep your variegation vibrant, provide the plant with more light. If the leaves don't have high margins of pink, offer more light, or propagate. Water your Pink Princess when you notice the soil is halfway to fully dry. The leaves will curl when extra thirsty. Plant your Pink Princess in a well-draining, chunky soil mixture that allows the roots to breathe between waterings. Fertilize regularly during the growing season.

Tip: Sometimes cutting a plant where variegation stops will encourage variegation to form on new growth shoots.

PITCHER PLANT/MONKEY CUPS

Nepenthes alata

Size: Up to 1 foot tall   **Growth Habit:** Upright   **Cost Rating:** $

PET FRIENDLY

The Pitcher Plant—native to parts of Southeast Asia, Madagascar, and Australia—is a carnivorous plant that eats live insects such as flies and gnats. Large, pitcher-shaped leaf modifications called pitfall traps are this plant's defining feature. The "pitchers" are typically red and green in color with red speckles.

Care: Some Pitcher Plants require full sun, whereas others need filtered light; the conditions depend on the species you have. Read the care tag or talk with a nursery employee to determine which one you have. Like most carnivorous plants, the Pitcher Plant likes soil that remains evenly moist, but not soaked. Plant in a low-nutrient mixture that retains moisture yet allows the roots to breathe. You can choose soil or a mixture of moss and perlite. This plant requires distilled or rain water, as well as high humidity of at least 50 percent.

Tip: Your Pitcher Plant should naturally catch insects without your help, but if none are around, feel free to feed the plant once or twice a month with a freshly killed fly.

POLKA-DOT BEGONIA
Begonia maculata wightii

Size: Up to 2+ feet tall **Growth Habit:** Upright **Cost Rating:** $$

NOT PET FRIENDLY

The Polka-Dot Begonia is a type of cane Begonia that grows thick stalks. This variety has long leaves with pointed tips and silvery-white polka dots. New leaves come in tiny and orange and grow to have deep green fronts and red backs.

Care: Begonias generally do well with humidity above 40 percent, which prevents brown tips and helps with consistent growth. The Polka-Dot Begonia enjoys high light such as in a south-facing window and can even handle a little direct morning sun. This plant doesn't like to dry out completely, so water thoroughly when you notice the soil is dry 2 to 3 inches down. Provide a well-draining soil mixture that allows for longer moisture retention. Consider planting in a ceramic or plastic pot to help prevent moisture from wicking away.

Did You Know: The Begonia genus is recognized as having more than 1,000 named species that are easy to hybridize—there are probably many more species than those already named.

RED PRAYER PLANT
Maranta leuconeura var. erythroneura

Size: Up to 6+ inches tall   **Growth Habit:** Creeping, Trailing   **Cost Rating:** $

PET FRIENDLY

The Red Prayer Plant is among the easiest to care for of the Marantaceae family. This plant is vocal when expressing its needs, though these are relatively few. The Red Prayer Plant is known for a unique ovate leaf pattern that features bright red pinstripes with light green splotches down the center. At night, this plant folds its leaves upward revealing their dark purple undersides, a protection that helps the plant remain undetected on the rainforest floor.

Care: The Red Prayer Plant is happy to live pulled back from all windows in indirect light. Let your Red Prayer Plant dry out 1 to 3 inches down before saturating the soil. Plant in a well-draining and chunky soil mixture containing additives like perlite or pumice, which allows for drainage as well as moisture retention. This plant can grow quickly in ideal conditions and enjoys spreading out horizontally, reflecting the natural propensity to creep across the rainforest floor.

Tip: To see your Red Prayer Plant in action, set up a time-lapse camera for a few hours in the morning to watch the plant come down from prayer position and dance the morning away.

REGAL SHIELD
Alocasia odora x reginula

Size: Up to 4+ feet tall **Growth Habit:** Upright **Cost Rating:** $$

NOT PET FRIENDLY

The Regal Shield is a cross between the *Alocasia odora* and *Alocasia reginula* and has large, dark, fan-like leaves.

Care: To care for the Regal Shield, place in bright indirect light in an east- or west-facing window or pulled back from a south-facing exposure. Straight from the nursery, this plant likely won't tolerate direct light unless slowly acclimated to higher light. Plant your Regal Shield in a light and airy soil mixture that allows for ample drainage. This plant enjoys drying out a little between waterings, but not for too long. Water thoroughly to evenly saturate. Fertilize regularly in the growing season.

RUBBER PLANT
Ficus elastica

Size: Up to 6+ feet tall   **Growth Habit:** Upright   **Cost Rating:** $$

NOT PET FRIENDLY

The Rubber Plant grows beautifully in the home. Though coming in several varieties that vary in variegation, each variety shares the shiny, waxy rubber-like leaves. Although sometimes tricky in the beginning, Rubber Plants will reward you with their beauty.

Care: With all Rubber Plants, high light is preferred from an east-, west-, or south-facing window. Darker foliage can handle darker lighting conditions. Make sure to plant in well-draining soil because the roots need room to breathe. Wait until the soil is almost completely dried out before thoroughly watering the plant. Use organic fertilizer once a month during the growing season to ensure healthy new growth.

Tip: This plant is a bit of a dust collector, so wash the leaves with a microfiber cloth when you water to ensure they can breathe and photosynthesize.

STAGHORN FERN

Platycerium bifurcatum

Size: Varies **Growth Habit:** Epiphyte (Mounted) **Cost Rating:** $$

PET FRIENDLY

The Staghorn Fern, most commonly found in Australia, is an incredibly unique houseplant with two types of leaves: antler fronds and shield fronds. The shield fronds grow around the root ball to protect the base of the plant. These fronds normally dry up and turn brown, eventually falling off.

Care: Staghorn Ferns are different from other ferns because they enjoy high amounts of light. Place your Staghorn Fern in an east- or west-facing window to receive bright indirect light, away from direct sun. To water this plant, soak it in water until the root ball is completely saturated. The fronds also capture water, so mist the plant periodically. On average, you will likely need to water your Staghorn Fern about once a week in the summertime. This plant also benefits from higher humidity areas. Because the Staghorn Fern should be mounted on a treated wood board to grow, soil is not needed. Wrap the roots in moss and fasten this mass to the board with fishing line. The mounting wood should be treated to withstand moisture to prevent rot. The plant should be watered by soaking the board and allowing it to dry for a few hours before replacing it on the wall.

STRAWBERRY BEGONIA

Saxifraga stolonifera

Size: Up to 1 foot long   **Growth Habit:** Bushy, Trailing   **Cost Rating:** $

NOT PET FRIENDLY

The Strawberry Begonia is not actually a member of the Begonia genus but of the Saxifraga genus. These plants shoot out babies from long stems, similar to the habits of Spider Plants (page 112). They have round, hairy leaves with pink stems.

Care: The Strawberry Begonia enjoys bright indirect light in an east- or west-facing window away from harsh sun rays. Choose a well-draining soil that still retains some moisture. Don't drench the leaves when watering, although they would be okay if they got wet. The Strawberry Begonia is happy to dry out between waterings, so water when the soil is almost or completely dried out.

> **Tip:** Place the Strawberry Begonia babies into cups of water around the mother plant while they are still attached. Doing so will help them grow a root system and be ready to be planted as soon as they're removed from their mother.

STRING OF PEARLS
Curio rowleyanus

Size: Up to 2+ feet tall   **Growth Habit:** Trailing   **Cost Rating:** $

NOT PET FRIENDLY

The String of Pearls is a lovely plant that grows in long vines of succulent pearls. In nature, this native of southwest Africa trails along the ground, forming a thick ground cover.

Care: The String of Pearls is a classic hanging succulent needing a few hours of bright direct light in a south-facing window. With the sun stress of high amounts of light, the leaves might even turn pink. Plant in an extremely well-draining and chunky soil mixture best suited for cactus and succulents. To allow the roots to fully dry out, water about once a month. It is a sign that you need to water sooner if the pearls shrivel and fall off.

Tip: To keep your String of Pearls looking thick from top to bottom, grab a few strands and coil them around the top of the plant. They will eventually take root.

STRING OF TURTLES
Peperomia prostrata

Size: Up to 1 foot long   **Growth Habit:** Creeping, Trailing   **Cost Rating:** $$

PET FRIENDLY

The String of Turtles is a trailing Peperomia native to Ecuador. The pattern on the leaves resembles a turtle shell, thus the name. Though most Peperomia are quite hardy, this one is much more sensitive with thin stems and small, round leaves.

Care: This plant does not need high amounts of light; in fact, best is low to moderate light in a north-facing window or pulled back from an east- or west-facing exposure. Water your String of Turtles when the soil is beginning to dry out; this plant does not like to be in drought too long. Plant in a well-draining soil mixture that allows for quick drainage while also encouraging moisture retention. Propagate String of Turtles by laying the plant flat against moss or removing the lower leaves and placing them in water.

Tip: You can grow this plant in a pot of your choosing or mount it onto a board.

SWISS CHEESE VINE/FIVE HOLES PLANT
Monstera adansonii

Size: Up to 3 feet tall   **Growth Habit:** Climbing, Trailing   **Cost Rating:** $–$$

NOT PET FRIENDLY

The Swiss Cheese Vine is one of the many members of the Monstera genus but is unique in having hole fenestrations from a young age. This plant comes in wide, narrow, or regular forms, and all are beautiful in their own way. Let the plant cascade down a bookshelf or grow up a moss pole and see how big the leaves can get.

Care: This trailing plant needs significant light and would do best in an east-facing window or pulled back from a south- or west-facing one. The plant likes ambient humidity but doesn't absolutely have to be in a humid setting. Use a chunky, well-draining soil mixture typical for aroids. Don't let this plant dry out completely between waterings; rather, let the soil dry about two-thirds of the way and then water deeply. If you notice your plant is getting leggy, prune to promote bushier growth.

Tip: To keep the Swiss Cheese Vine looking full and bushy, cut under a node and place the cutting in water or a propagation medium until the roots are a few inches in length. Once the cuttings are finished rooting, dig a small hole in the pot and plant them.

UMBRELLA PLANT/OCTOPUS PLANT

Schefflera actinophylla

Size: Up to 3+ feet tall   **Growth Habit:** Upright   **Cost Rating:** $

NOT PET FRIENDLY

As the name suggests, the Umbrella Plant can be identified by clusters of leaves that resemble the round shape of umbrellas, usually grown in eight leaflets per cluster. The Umbrella Plant comes in regular, dwarf, all-green, and variegated forms. Generally, if allowed, this plant will grow quite tall and fill up a corner.

Care: To keep your Umbrella Plant bushy, place it in bright indirect light in an east- or west-facing window away from harsh sun rays. Providing the plant with enough light will prevent it from stretching out. The all-green variety can handle lower light conditions than the variegated. Let the plant dry out about halfway before watering. Choose a soil that is well-draining and include additives like coco chips and pumice.

Did You Know: A juvenile Umbrella Plant stem will produce clusters with as few as five leaflets. With maturation, the leaflets will go up to eight.

VENUS FLY TRAP
Dionaea muscipula

Size: Up to 5 inches tall   **Growth Habit:** Upright   **Cost Rating:** $

PET FRIENDLY

The Venus Fly Trap is a carnivorous plant, eating live bugs such as fruit flies, house flies, or crickets. These wonderfully interactive plants are native to subtropical wetlands. This environment can be tricky to replicate indoors, but with the right tools, your Venus Fly Trap will thrive.

Care: The most important part of caring for a Venus Fly Trap is keeping the soil evenly moist but not soggy. Water from below with distilled or rain water, because other types of water contain too many minerals. This plant needs high amounts of light and humidity, so place this plant near a south-facing window and in a humid place. Use a nutrient-rich soil mixture made from coco peat, sphagnum moss, and/or perlite. Venus Fly Traps will catch bugs on their own, but if yours is in an enclosed environment and cannot do so, feed one live bug to one of the heads about once a month. Stop feeding during winter months.

Did You Know: The Venus Fly Trap takes about a week to digest a bug.

WATERMELON DISCHIDIA
Dischidia ovata

Size: Up to 2+ feet tall   **Growth Habit:** Trailing   **Cost Rating:** $

PET FRIENDLY

The Watermelon Dischidia is a small-leaved, trailing plant. The name comes from the watermelon-like patterning and coloring of the green oval leaves with thin white stripes down the center. This plant is part of the Dischidia genus, a diverse group of epiphytic plants common to parts of New Guinea, Australia, and East Asia.

Care: The Watermelon Dischidia enjoys bright light close to an east-, west- or south-facing window but doesn't necessarily need direct light; indirect bright light in an east- or west-facing window would also make this plant happy. Let the soil dry out completely between waterings because the thick succulent-like leaves are wonderful water reservoirs. As an epiphyte, this plant enjoys a chunkier soil mixture with plenty of room for the roots to breathe and water to run through.

Did You Know: With high amounts of light, this plant becomes sun-stressed and the leaves turn pink.

WATERMELON PEPEROMIA/WATERMELON BEGONIA

Peperomia argyreia

Size: Up to 6 inches tall   **Growth Habit:** Bushy   **Cost Rating:** $$

PET FRIENDLY

The Watermelon Peperomia is sure to turn heads with light green foliage and silvery stripes that resemble the pattern seen on a watermelon. Juicy leaves serve as a reservoir for water and are good indicators of what the plant needs. All Peperomia are pet-safe.

Care: This sensitive plant is best suited to being pulled back from bright windows, as direct light can burn the leaves. The thick, succulent leaves and stems will indicate thirst when you are able to bend the leaves without snapping them. Choose well-draining soil that allows the water to easily run through.

Tip: To propagate by stem-cutting, cut the stem 3 or 4 inches from a healthy leaf, providing enough length to reach into a glass of water. To propagate by leaf-cutting, cut a healthy leaf in half horizontally, add rooting hormone to the cut side, and place it into your propagation medium. Keep your growing medium moist but not wet for best results. The waiting game will be worth the trouble.

Chapter 8

HIGH-MAINTENANCE PLANTS

BIRD OF PARADISE

Strelitzia reginae

Size: Up to 4+ feet tall **Growth Habit:** Upright **Cost Rating:** $$

NOT PET FRIENDLY

The Bird of Paradise is best known for its large, long leaves. You'll see these plants growing naturally in tropical to subtropical regions, but they can also be grown inside under certain conditions. When they are happiest, they will produce orange or white flowers that resemble a bird flying.

Care: The Bird of Paradise needs a vast amount of light, such as in a south-facing window or even outside on the patio. They are most likely to flower in high light. In such light, they will likely also need to be watered more often than other plants. Keep the soil evenly moist during the growing season. The soil should always be well-draining with soil additives that help the roots breathe, like perlite, pumice, and coco chips. Fertilize every 2 weeks during the growing season for continued growth and flowering.

Tip: Wash the leaves with a mixture of 1 part water and 1 part lemon juice and use a microfiber cloth. Doing so will help cut through watermarks and remove residual dust.

CALATHEA NETWORK
Goeppertia kegeljanii

Size: Up to 6 inches tall   **Growth Habit:** Bushy, Trailing   **Cost Rating:** $$

PET FRIENDLY

The signature feature of the Calathea Network (formerly *Calathea musaica*) is its intricate leaf design, a mosaic pattern with millions of lines and dashes. This plant is a member of the prayer plant family (Marantaceae) and will fold up at night.

Care: Because the Calathea Network prefers moderate to low light and will not do well in high-light conditions, place it back from bright windows. Use distilled or filtered water because the leaves are quite sensitive and will get excess brown tips or edges with other types of water. When the soil is about halfway dry, water. Fertilize this plant about every other time you water for best results.

CROTON PETRA
Codiaeum variegatum

Size: Up to 2+ feet tall   **Growth Habit:** Upright   **Cost Rating:** $

NOT PET FRIENDLY

The Croton Petra is the most common Croton variety, best known for large leaves that vary in color. Most striking are the bright yellow and orange leaves with small flecks of green.

Care: The Croton Petra is no stranger to dropping leaves when unhappy. Keep your plant in one place in direct sunlight in a south-facing window for up to 6 hours a day to keep growth full. Following these guidelines will ensure the colors stay vibrant. The Croton Petra is pretty vocal and will droop low when thirsty. Plant it in a well-draining and chunky soil mixture. Root rot begins to set in when this plant's roots are allowed to stay wet for too long.

Did You Know: The Croton is an evergreen, native to Southern Asia and other Pacific Islands.

MAIDENHAIR FERN
Adiantum (genus)

Size: Up to 6 inches tall   **Growth Habit:** Bushy   **Cost Rating:** $

PET FRIENDLY

The Maidenhair Fern is a coveted fern with delicate fronds and bushy growth. Each frond features small, delicate, round leaves that are soft to the touch. This plant is more finicky because of specific watering and humidity needs—after all, the Maidenhair Fern is most often found growing on rock walls behind waterfalls!

Care: The Maidenhair Fern, like most ferns, does not need lots of light. The low indirect light of a north-facing window, pulled away from harsh sun rays and heat, is best. This plant needs high humidity to maintain foliage. If the humidity drops, you will likely soon notice the plant's leaves falling or turning crispy. The soil needs to maintain moisture without staying soggy. Water your Maidenhair Fern when the soil dries out even a bit so the soil stays moist, and make sure water drains out the drainage hole. Fertilize with a weak fertilizer mixture once a month.

Tip: The Maidenhair Fern is a wonderful plant to water by wicking (see page 30) with continuous access to water.

PHILODENDRON VERRUCOSUM

Philodendron hybrid

Size: Up to 5+ feet tall   **Growth Habit:** Upright   **Cost Rating:** $$$

NOT PET FRIENDLY

The Philodendron Verrucosum is a delicate, velvet-leaf plant. With leaves that are quite thin, this plant is less likely to hold on to water for long. This variety is harder to find depending on where you live. Provided with the right circumstances, this plant grows wonderfully and is worth the search.

Care: Because of its thin leaves, the Philodendron Verrucosum needs to be monitored more closely than other Philodendron varieties. This plant thrives in high humidity and will brown and crisp without enough moisture. The leaves will wilt and curl when the plant is thirsty, but water before this point to ensure the best leaf health. Use a moss pole or bamboo stake to allow the plant to climb up.

Tip: Velcro plant ties are wonderful tools to tether the plant to the pole and encourage upward growth because they are much more delicate on the stems than string or rope.

STROMANTHE TRIOSTAR
Stromanthe sanguinea

Size: Up to 1+ feet tall   **Growth Habit:** Upright   **Cost Rating:** $$

PET FRIENDLY

The Stromanthe Triostar is a striking member of the Marantaceae family with bright, eye-catching colors on the tops of the leaves and dark reds on the bottoms. The leaves are long and can be green, light green, pink, or white. Each leaf looks hand-painted.

Care: The high humidity needs of the Stromanthe Triostar makes this plant difficult to care for. With a tendency to be quite unforgiving by nature, this plant is happiest when pulled away from any bright windows and placed in a more shaded part of your home. The Stromanthe Triostar prefers to be watered with filtered or distilled water to prevent leaf burn; brown leaf edges are common for this plant and indicate something is wrong. Plant your Triostar in a moisture-holding, but quick-draining, soil mixture heavy in coco peat.

Tip: To help your Triostar maintain beautiful, lush foliage, place it under a cloche to serve as a humidity dome indefinitely or temporarily.

VELVET CARDBOARD ANTHURIUM
Anthurium clarinervium

Size: Up to 2+ feet tall   **Growth Habit:** Upright   **Cost Rating:** $$$$

NOT PET FRIENDLY

The Velvet Cardboard Anthurium is a striking, velvet-leaf tropical plant best known for its deep green color and bright white-ish veining. Although much easier to find today than previously, this plant is not exactly the easiest to take care of. Even so, new leaves bring great reward as they emerge as small and rust-colored and mature into majestic, deep green masterpieces.

Care: With darker leaves, the Velvet Cardboard Anthurium does not need high light. This plant would do well pulled back from a north- or east-facing window. Use a well-draining, chunky soil mixture that you don't allow to dry out, and pay particular attention to humidity conditions. Without ambient humidity of greater than 50 percent, the Velvet Cardboard Anthurium will more quickly use moisture from the soil and the oldest leaves.

Tip: For best results and to avoid leaf burn, consider watering with distilled or reverse osmosis water.

RESOURCES

ASPCA

ASPCA.org/pet-care/animal-poison-control/toxic-and-non-toxic-plants

The ASPCA created this resource for plant and pet parents to gain a better understanding of which plants are toxic and what to do when a toxic plant has been ingested.

Bloom and Grow Radio Podcast

BloomAndGrowRadio.com

On this podcast hosted by Maria Fallia, experts discuss topics like watering, natural light, and soil science.

***Houseplants for All: How to Fill Any House with Happy Plants* by Danae Horst**

This book provides tips on plant care and choosing the right plant for your lifestyle.

Plant Care Today

PlantCareToday.com

This website covers houseplants and outdoor plants.

Summer Rayne Oakes's YouTube Channel

YouTube.com/user/summerrayneoakes

An environmental scientist and houseplant expert, Summer shares her wide range of houseplant knowledge on her YouTube channel.

***Wild at Home* by Hilton Carter**

This book teaches readers how to fill their spaces with plants as a key design element.

REFERENCES

ASPCA. *Poisonous Plants*. ASPCA.org/pet-care/animal-poison-control/toxic
-and-non-toxic-plants.

Bratman, Gregory N., Christopher B. Anderson, Marc G. Berman, Bobby Cochran,
Sjerp de Vries, Jon Flanders, Carl Folke, et al. "Nature and Mental Health: An
Ecosystem Service Perspective." *Science Advances* 5, no. 7 (July 24, 2019),
doi.org/10.1126/sciadv.aax0903.

Dela Cruz, Majbrit, Jan H. Christensen, Jane Dyrhauge Thomsen, and Renate
Müller. "Can Ornamental Potted Plants Remove Volatile Organic Compounds
from Indoor Air?" *Environmental Science and Pollution Research* 21, no. 24
(July 25, 2014): 13909–13928, doi.org/10.1007/s11356-014-3240-x.

Robbins, Jim. "Ecopsychology: How Immersion in Nature Benefits Your
Health." *Yale Environment 360* (January 9, 2020), E360.Yale.edu/features
/ecopsychology-how-immersion-in-nature-benefits-your-health.

White, Matthew P., Ian Alcock, James Grellier, Benedict W. Wheeler, Terry Hartig,
Sara L. Warber, Angie Bone, et al. "Spending at Least 120 Minutes a Week in
Nature Is Associated with Good Health and Wellbeing." *Scientific Reports* 9,
no. 1 (June 13, 2019): 7730, doi.org/10.1038/s41598-019-44097-3.

Wolverton, B.C, Anne Johnson, and Keith Bounds. "Interior Landscape Plants
for Indoor Air Pollution Abatement." NASA NTRS (September 15, 1989),
NTRS.NASA.gov/citations/19930073077.

GLOSSARY

aroid: the name for the Araceae plant family

cultivar: the cultivated variety of a plant that was produced through cross-pollination and that is not *usually* found in nature unless by mutation

epiphyte: a non-parasitic plant that grows along or on another plant, usually a tree

fenestrations: the natural holes in leaves

foliar: relating to leaves

genus: a taxonomic category that defines a group of organisms with strong similarities

node: the point on a stem from which buds, leaves, and branches grow

propagate: the process of creating plants from existing plant material

root ball: the collective roots that grow beneath the soil

spadix: the part of the aroid flower, a spike at the center of the spathe, from which pollen will form

spathe: the sheath growing around the spadix or flower cluster; it is a modified leaf called a bract

substrate: the substance from which a plant grows

terrestrial: native to soil

trailing: hanging; dangling; creeping

transpiration: the process by which plants absorb moisture from the soil and release it into the air

variegation: two or more colors on a leaf in a varying or repeated pattern

INDEX

ACKNOWLEDGMENTS

My online plant friends, the people from whom I learn the most every day.
My husband, for loving me and tolerating my plants.
My mom, for encouraging me to always challenge myself.
Callisto Media, for believing in my potential.

ABOUT THE AUTHOR

Rebecca De La Paz is a plant enthusiast and collector from the desert Southwest. She began her journey with plants at a young age, but after graduating from the University of Arizona with a BA in English literature, she was pulled toward houseplants. Through extensive research, observation, and trial and error, she has developed a keen sense for what plants need. Rebecca has been interviewed on podcasts, featured on the news, and interviewed by plant publications. She shares her knowledge on her YouTube channel, Becca De La Plants, and her website, IndoorJungleDirectory.delaplants.com. You can find her on Instagram @delaplants.

CPSIA information can be obtained
at www.ICGtesting.com
Printed in the USA
JSHW021435061122
32696JS00001B/1

9 781647 398507